# INTUITION @
# WORK

## About the Author

Melanie Barnum (Bethel, CT) is a psychic, medium, intuitive counselor, life coach, and hypnotist who has been practicing professionally for more than twenty years. She was a VIP Reader at Psych Out, a gathering of the nation's foremost psychics, organized by Court TV. Barnum is also an Angelspeake Facilitator, a member of the National Guild of Hypnotists (NGH), and the International Association of Counselors and Therapists (IACT).

# INTUITION@
# WORK

## Trust your Gut to Get Ahead in Business & in Life

## MELANIE BARNUM

Llewellyn Publications
Woodbury, Minnesota

FIRST EDITION
First Printing, 2021

Book design by Donna Burch-Brown
Cover design by Shira Atakpu

Llewellyn Publications is a registered trademark of Llewellyn Worldwide Ltd.

**Library of Congress Cataloging-in-Publication Data**
Names: Barnum, Melanie, author.
Title: Intuition at work : trust your gut to get ahead in business and in
  life / Melanie Barnum.
Description: First edition. | Woodbury, Minnesota : Llewellyn Publications,
  [2021] | Includes bibliographical references. | Summary: "Through
  hands-on exercises, inspiring stories, and clever techniques, Melanie
  Barnum provides innovative ways to succeed in the workplace and in life,
  no matter your profession"— Provided by publisher.
Identifiers: LCCN 2020053590 (print) | LCCN 2020053591 (ebook) | ISBN
  9780738766331 (paperback) | ISBN 9780738766546 (ebook)
Subjects: LCSH: Intuition. | Success in business. | Success.
Classification: LCC BF315.5 .B36 2021 (print) | LCC BF315.5 (ebook) | DDC
  153.4/4—dc23
LC record available at https://lccn.loc.gov/2020053590
LC ebook record available at https://lccn.loc.gov/2020053591

Llewellyn Worldwide Ltd. does not participate in, endorse, or have any authority or responsibility concerning private business transactions between our authors and the public.

All mail addressed to the author is forwarded but the publisher cannot, unless specifically instructed by the author, give out an address or phone number.

Any internet references contained in this work are current at publication time, but the publisher cannot guarantee that a specific location will continue to be maintained. Please refer to the publisher's website for links to authors' websites and other sources.

Llewellyn Publications
A Division of Llewellyn Worldwide Ltd.
2143 Wooddale Drive
Woodbury, MN 55125-2989
www.llewellyn.com

Printed in the United States of America

## Also by Melanie Barnum

*The Book of Psychic Symbols*

*Llewellyn's Little Book of Psychic Development*

*Manifest Your Year*

*Psychic Abilities for Beginners*

*Psychic Abilities Beyond Beginners*

*Psychic Vision*

*The Steady Way to Greatness*

## Dedication

I have to give a shout-out to my entire family, yet again!

Tom and his morning tea support,

and Molly and Samantha for being my greatest-ever creations.

Tammy and Adam, my forever supporters.

And, a shout-out to all the hustlers and badasses who are trying everything

they can

to not just survive,

but to rise up

and take back their innate power of intuition—

this one's for you!

# Acknowledgments

Writing a book is such an interesting thing—just when you think you know exactly how it's going to go, you discover how incredibly wrong you are. Originally, I started out planning on not using any stories. That did not go as I thought it would—at all! I wanted to write a book that combined business life and personal life, that showed how intuition has no boundaries, and showed how we can better ourselves when we open up to our vast gifts in every area of our lives.

So, I definitely need to give a huge thanks to everyone who contributed stories of their own personal and business intuitive jewels of wisdom. The stories they shared were sometimes never heard before, and they've entrusted me to write them with the responsibility of reading them with an open mind and kindness. And a special thanks to the goddesses of Goddess Weekend who lifted me up with ideas and praise and encouraged me to write this book!

Thank you to all the people who supported my crazy writing schedule, my family and friends, and those who sent 2 a.m. texts to make sure I was okay, and the incredible editors at Llewellyn—shout-out to Angela Wix!

Also, a big thanks to all who, like me, want answers and keep searching for how it all works. I can't thank the seekers without thanking all those who give us answers. Thanks for all you're doing to continue paving the way with your books, your readings, your workshops, and, yes, your television shows.

It is the people who believe in intuition, and even who challenge us, who help propel us forward, so thank you!

# Disclaimer

The practices and techniques described in this book should not be used as an alternative to professional medical treatment. This book does not attempt to give medical diagnosis, treatment, prescriptions, or suggestions for medication in relation to any human disease, pain, injury, deformity, or physical or mental condition.

The author and publisher of this book are not responsible in any manner whatsoever for any injury that may occur through following the examples contained herein. It is recommended that you consult your physician to obtain a diagnosis for any physical or mental symptoms you may experience.

While the author intends for you to learn how to use your intuition at work, this book makes no guarantee that you will increase your wealth or profitability by following the recommended practices.

The stories shared in this book are based on real-life events and readings. The names and circumstances may have been changed to preserve privacy.

# Contents

# Exercises: Try This!

# Introduction

*When you reach the end of what you should know,*
*you will be at the beginning of what you should sense.*

—KAHLIL GIBRAN, *SAND AND FOAM*

"How can you possibly sell it if you don't advertise that you're selling it?" my employee Cara asked, with incredulity and frustration. "It really doesn't make any sense!"

We were standing at the counter of my children's store, talking about the possibility of selling it.

"I hear you, but I feel like I have to trust my intuition," I responded.

I had opened the store years ago, and in fact this was my second location. I had followed my intuition when I decided to switch careers and create this new business. Now, I was considering selling it. We were moving and I felt like I needed to have a fresh start and give my psychic career a real chance to blossom. It was time for the next phase of my life. But I had to sell the store first.

"I just don't get it. You're talking about trying to sell the store, but how are people going to know you are even offering it? It's impossible," Cara told me.

"I understand. It doesn't seem like it would make sense, but I feel it in my gut—it will work out!"

I thought about my intentions. I wanted to sell my store and had very particular ideas of what I needed. Though I wasn't sure how it would happen specifically, I intuitively knew it would. I wanted it to go to someone who would appreciate it like I did. After all, I had started the business from scratch and put a lot of love into it. I also needed to get a fair price, fair to both of us, and it needed to happen smoothly. I saw it happening in my mind like a handshake deal—smooth, honest, and easy. And, finally, it had to sell within four months. Again, I was moving and did not want to commute to work every day.

Cara continued looking at me like I'd lost my mind.

"Okay, but don't forget—I already have a new job lined up," she reminded me.

"Fine. I will put a sign up in the window." I capitulated, wondering like Cara how the heck would I reach an agreement with someone otherwise.

My logical mind was stepping in, trying to take over, so I listened to it, briefly, and made a sign for the window:

BUSINESS FOR SALE: INQUIRE WITHIN OR BY PHONE.

Soon after, I received a few inquiries in person and on the telephone. I talked to the potential buyers, and immediately we discovered they would not be the ones to buy it. During the week, I had a couple more calls asking for details. I knew, intuitively, without even calling them back, that these parties also would not be the one to buy it. They wouldn't love it or nurture it and it would fail.

"Listen, Melanie. This just doesn't make sense. How can you possibly be sure that you're not losing a sale by not returning their calls?" Cara questioned.

"I can't explain it to you. But I know, deep down, the right person is coming. And more than that, it will all work out exactly how it's supposed to," I told her.

I believed this so strongly that I actually took down the sign I had put up, while Cara shook her head laughing in disbelief. I was done explaining, though, because intuitively I knew it would be proven soon enough that the perfect situation was revving up to occur.

A few days later, someone came into the store. While they were shopping, they asked if I was still selling the store. I asked them how they knew it was for sale and if they were interested.

"At your previous location I remember you saying you might possibly want to sell it in the future at some point. My mother has always talked about wanting to open a children's consignment store like yours. This would be perfect. So, is this the future? Are you selling? My mom just retired from her job, and I'm pretty sure she is ready!"

It all happened so quickly after that. I wrote up a sales contract, and they purchased it within a month. We agreed on a fair price, and they loved it and nurtured it as I had. It was an ideal transaction and one that made me really happy.

I probably would have sold it eventually had I put an ad in the paper, but my intuition was telling me that wasn't the way to go. I felt strongly that I would manifest the right buyer with all the right details, and I'm so pleased with the way it all happened. Listening to my intuition contributed to my bottom line and my happiness, allowing everything to go smoothly. We won't always know the outcome if we don't follow our gut instincts in our business or personal lives, but we will always reap the benefits when we do, and more often than not, our intuition will steer us in a positive direction.

## Leveraging Your Intuition

If you could make your life easier, why wouldn't you? Everyone utilizes tools for a variety of life challenges and jobs, so why not use a tool that you have naturally? You have an intuitive ability, an innate gift available to tap into that can help you be your badass self, with absolutely no apologies. No more waiting. You don't need an engraved invitation, and you certainly don't need to wait until you screw something up. That would be self-sabotaging at its finest. Well, that's not happening—not this time. You've picked up this book, so you're obviously curious. There's no turning back. You're ready. You are going to be more successful than you can imagine—not just in business but in your entire life! It's time to leverage your intuition.

What exactly does it mean to leverage your intuition? Good question. When you leverage something, you are exerting some sort of influence or power over something else in order to make something better or to benefit in some way. When you leverage your intuition to increase your business acumen, you are simply using your gut instincts to help you get ahead. It doesn't matter if the business skills you are trying to enhance are corporate, public, private, communal, or even personal; this is your life, so it's time to rock it. When you use your natural gifts, you'll discover how to get ahead without having to manipulate or step on others, creating mutually beneficial relationships. And when you utilize the (possibly) greatest tool you have, it increases the odds that you will succeed.

But how can we leverage something we don't fully understand? First, you need to know what intuition is. Intuition is instinctive. It's an intrinsic capacity to know things, through our extrasensory perception, without any concrete or conscious reason. Intuition flows through us and is already part of our lives. Sherrie Dillard, author and professional psychic, knows that "everyone is intuitive and can further develop the ability to access their most natural and innate wisdom."[1] It's not so much whether we are intuitive or not; rather, it's how we acknowledge it. It can show up as a gentle murmur, or it can be persistent and almost annoying, like it's shouting at you to listen.

Intuition has many names. Sometimes we refer to it as a parent's intuition and describe it as the almost telepathic connection a mother or father has with their child at times. We've heard of a cop's hunch. They may not call it intuition, but they will say it is good, crime-solving instinct. And, of course, there is the word *psychic*, which for some can conjure up images of crystal balls, flowy scarves, and giant hoop earrings but in reality is actually a more highly developed sense of intuition.

I often use the word *psychic* interchangeably with *intuitive*. While this is not totally incorrect, the two words don't mean exactly the same thing. Intuition is something we are all born with. It is part of our natural birthright. It is something we can count on to help guide us and keep us going on the right

---

1. Sherrie Dillard, *You Are Psychic: Develop Your Natural Intuition through Your Psychic Type* (Woodbury, MN: Llewellyn Publications, 2018), 16.

path toward success. Psychic ability is the same thing and then some. It is a more advanced sense that goes beyond the normal intuitive gifts. Possessed by some, it is a natural propensity to have a next-level talent with extrasensory perception. Think of it this way: Whether or not we're on key doesn't matter. For the most part we can all sing a note. However, it doesn't mean we will be Andrea Bocelli or Beyoncé.

I am a professional psychic and use my gifts to help people all around the world by tuning in to their lives. You too may aspire to be a professional psychic, or, more likely, you might be tuning in to your gifts to use them in business or in your personal life. Whichever way you are inclined, learning when and where to tap into your potential can get you started.

## When to Use Intuition

When should you use your intuition? Always! There really is never a reason to shut it down and turn it off. Laura Day, author, intuitive, and business coach, writes, "Intuition can empower you to be productive and active in any situation."[2] When you meet a new person and need to know who they are at their core, tune in to it. When you need to lessen risk while taking chances, you know it—tune in to your vibes. And, of course, tune in to manifest what you want! Tap into it during any type of life changes, from relationships in your personal life and business to moving around the world. How could you make such significant and meaningful changes without utilizing your metaphysical senses? When you are trying to get ahead in business, it can provide you with a leg up. Intuition helps you make better choices and directs you to make better decisions. The real question should be, when wouldn't you use your intuition? It is powerful beyond measure.

You know how it feels if you've ignored that feeling down deep in your gut—when you've disregarded that whisper inside telling you something would not work out. You know you've messed up. You can feel it in your bones, and you tell yourself, "Why didn't I pay attention? I knew this wouldn't be a good situation!" Yup, that's regret. It's the abysmal knowing that you

---

2. Laura Day, *Practical Intuition: How to Harness the Power of Your Instinct and Make It Work for You* (New York: Broadway Books, 1997), 12.

missed an opportunity. It's what happens when you don't listen to your intuition, and you feel like you obliterated every chance you have to succeed. I agree with Lisa Earle McLeod, author, leadership consultant, and keynote speaker, when she writes, "When you ignore your instincts, and go forward despite a slightly uncomfortable feeling in your gut, you almost always regret it."[3] This is why, instead, you need to use your intuition—always!

Intuition doesn't care about preference. It doesn't care what you like or even what you want. Intuition is true north. It's the feeling that's backed with centuries of ancestral knowledge. Intuition doesn't care about what's popular or what's trendy. Intuition calls you out on all your BS by making you feel off or uncomfortable when you are not doing the right thing. It tries to gently guide you toward your power without hitting too many potholes along the way. Intuition says, "Pay attention to me!" because if you don't, the ripples you create will have consequences in your future.

Intuition is nonlinear. It doesn't have a step-by-step guide that you have to follow before you can tap into it. Once you've absorbed and become relatively comfortable with the basics of how intuition works, you can move on to the practicalities of discovering the myriad of ways it can help you grow. Unlike taking classes at school, there are no prerequisites needed to move from one subject to another. Instead, you can think of it as kind of making lateral moves as you develop your gifts.

Maybe you've noticed your intuition at work already. Possibly, you've had an intuitive wake-up call and been surprised when your gifts showed up, or you've gradually noticed your instincts kicking in. It's possible you haven't felt it appear in your life so far but you've gathered that intuition could provide an advantage to help you get ahead. You can be confident all the above are fantastic. There's no wrong time to follow your curiosity and dig in, and you certainly don't need a huge, life-altering event to change your trajectory—unless, of course, that's what brought you here.

---

3. Lisa Earle McLeod, "How to Leverage Intuition in Decision-Making," HuffPost, last modified November 24, 2014, https://www.huffpost.com/entry/how-to-leverage-intuition_b_5868488.

# Who Am I to Tell You?

I am a professional psychic, via the life-altering moment. I am one of those people who needed to be hit over the head, almost literally. I scoffed at the self-helpers, the ones who believed in the woo-woo part of life. I've always been intuitive, and I "read" people even before I knew I was doing at. However, I was never comfortable with being one of the sheep, one of the group of followers who believed in something just because someone told me to believe it. I was too controlling, and I knew it. I was the one who went into a reading with a psychic, whether it was a boardwalk, $10 palm reading or a $200 in-person session with someone others loved and gushed about, and wouldn't say a word. I sat there with my arms crossed, doubting everything that came out of their mouths. I would (much later, of course) process what they said and determine whether it was specific enough to fit into what I wanted for my life, because God forbid, they told me something I didn't like.

Before I found my true calling as a professional psychic, life coach, hypnotist, and energy healer, I was an accountant, the controller of a company, and the owner/operator of a boutique store, in that order. I am, you see, quite balanced. I am left and right brained at the same time, meaning I am part logic and part woo-woo—or more specifically, intuitive and creative. I always believed in intuition; I just never realized how often I used it in business because, after all, it was natural for me and I didn't really analyze it that much.

Over twenty years ago, I was standing in my dining room, waiting for my sister to return to talk about the psychic reading she'd just had. Tammy had left her one-year-old with me and my newborn to go have a session with someone who wanted to teach a workshop at her healing center, and she wanted to see if the psychic was legit. The plan was that she'd go first, and if she was good, then Tammy would make an appointment for me to go see her next. Well, before that happened, I had a life-changing moment.

I had just put down my daughter and felt like I was literally hit over the head, and I heard the words, "You need to do this work now." It was not a loud voice, but rather it was quiet and gentle. At the same time, it was very authoritative, and it instantly gave me the impression that I had to listen. With just those words, the message could have meant anything, but I knew, in the bottom of my soul, what it meant. I just didn't believe it. I couldn't contemplate being told to become a professional psychic.

How was that possible? I couldn't just hang a shingle outside my door that said PSYCHIC. No way was I going to do that—or so I thought. I had always been somewhat intuitive. I'd read people, thinking that's what everyone did, but I didn't know that what I did was beyond the norm. Well, that was really my first big wake-up call with my intuition. I realized almost immediately that I was drawn to the possibility, in a huge way, so I set out to learn everything I possibly could about tapping into my intuition, and for me, that also meant remembering intuitive hits I had previously disregarded. And there were a lot.

When I was young, in my early teens, I had a vision in which I saw myself owning a boutique. It was a smallish, brightly colored boutique that I felt I had created from scratch. I figured it was a mistake because I was not into fashion, nor could I see myself going into the city to be a buyer. Fast-forward to the days after that vision and prior to the revelation that I should do psychic work, and I found myself standing in the middle of my new store, a children's consignment boutique, and it hit me—I owned a brightly colored boutique! It didn't occur to me before that moment that it was exactly what I saw in my vision. I wasn't in denial, per se. I just hadn't recognized it yet for what it was. It took a while to set in. This memory helped convince me of the importance of using my intuition in business.

Trusting my intuition had come into play with actually opening my new boutique as well, though, again, I didn't think much of it at the time. Before I quit my job as the controller of a company, I began thinking of what I could do to enable myself to be with my soon-to-be daughter and got the idea of opening the store, but I couldn't decide. I tried to tap into my intuition, knowing I'd always had some kind of awareness, but I had no trust in my abilities. I thought my gut was telling me to quit and go for it, but I needed confirmation to actually trust that I really had tapped into my intuition. So I asked for a sign. I essentially said, "Show me something that will let me believe my vibes are real."

A couple of days went by and I was in my office with my coworker. She was pregnant as well, due the next day. As she was walking by, I saw a little person walking next to her against the wall. The person I saw beside her had my coworker's blonde hair and blue eyes but her husband's features—same nose and face shape. I was taken aback for a second until I realized I was seeing the child who was to come. Sure enough, the next day the baby was born exactly as I had seen her. I realized that was my rapid confirmation my intuition was working, and soon after, I gave my notice and left to open my store.

I had it for a few years and then followed my intuition to sell it, incredible as it was, and became a professional psychic and healer. Now, with a couple of decades and numerous books under my belt, I am convinced that although I was surprised by the way it happened, I am on the right path to consistently opening myself to my ever-increasing abilities, and I am doing the work I was directed to do. I am confident that having listened to my gut instincts, I made the smart decision.

I proceeded to follow my gut instincts and signed up for classes and workshops to get me started on my journey. I realized that I had a propensity for the work and offered free readings for years until I felt comfortable enough with my gifts to become a professional.

So who am I to tell you how to leverage your intuition? To make this worthwhile, I'd better have something to offer you. And I do. I know what it means to use your intuitive abilities to help you attain your goals, and I teach people all over the world how to do just that.

## Are You Full?

Do you have the wisdom to take the chance and change your life? Are you full of desire to reach your next business goal? Are you full of hope that what you're doing could actually help you this time? Are you ready to finally trust that you're an instinctive being who may also be powerful enough to sway the business minds of others by combining your learned, professional knowledge with your natural, inherent gifts? Are you full of enough want to give yourself the opportunity to actually thrive in business? If you've answered yes to all of these, you are definitely full of it, and in a great way! If not, let's be honest: you're lying to yourself.

We all want to succeed. We all want to live a prosperous and happy life, and—let's face it—we want to be triumphant. We lie to ourselves about what we want because of the fear we may have that we can't succeed or make it to the top because we are not good enough, not smart enough, not funny enough, not good-looking enough, not strong enough, not liked enough, not connected enough, or most importantly, just not deserving enough. I am here to tell you that voice that holds you back, that rope that is pulling you back into the bowels of your own life, is bullshit. You can control it, quiet it down, cut yourself free from the boundaries, and soar. You are full of everything you need to achieve it all.

We can have whatever we wish for. Really, it can happen! When we believe in the possibility enough, we can manifest it all. Though manifestation is not the same as intuition, it is like anything else—you can miss out on the opportunity to create what you want if you ignore your own abilities. So for no other reason, maybe, than for your own sake, put aside any negativity and open your mind to what can be an amazing gift. Manifesting is an important aspect of believing in the powerful connections we have to each other and to life, and we can take advantage of this to a greater degree when we better comprehend our extrasensory gifts. Our intentions can absolutely direct what we create, but first we must believe we are worthy.

Why do so many of us believe we actually *can't* be enough? Why is it we feel we have to apologize when we achieve something maybe above or beyond what our friends may have accomplished? Possibly because we've been programmed to slow our roll; we don't want to get too full of ourselves. But why not? Why not be successful, and more importantly, why not use every tool, including intuitive tools, in our arsenal to do it? Your intuition is one of your strengths. It is something everyone has access to but not everyone utilizes. Why? Sometimes it's as simple as the disbelief that it can actually work or that intuition is real. Here's the deal: intuition is like your superpower. Would you apologize for that? I don't think so. You better be sure you're not apologizing for taking advantage of your natural intuitive gifts!

## What You Have to Look Forward To

We are in an age when developing one's intuition has become more common. This is partly because people are opening up naturally and partly because people realize the benefits of tuning in. There is an increase in the quest for knowledge—people want to know how to tune in for themselves and are reading more books on the topic and investing in workshops and teachers. You can pick out the right methods for you from those provided within these pages. From practicing using your intuitive senses to protecting yourself energetically, you'll find everything you need.

One main reason to jump in and develop your intuitive senses is so you can learn how to naturally read people, understanding where they are coming from and what motivates them. This will increase your leverage in business as well as your personal life. Knowing who you can trust can help you create and build relationships and partnerships. This gift will help strengthen and increase your power. It can also teach you the best way to win people over, in a good way, and even influence them, as well as alternatively listening to others when your intuition tells you that their ideas may be better. This knowledge, this ability, will also give you wisdom to know when to walk away from something or someone so you can welcome in better energy.

We've all heard of energy—the energy that runs our electricity or fuels our hot water (thank goodness for warm showers!) and the fuel that burns as energy to heat our homes and enable us to drive our cars. There's also the physical energy that we use to exercise or play sports. Some of us have so much energy we can run marathons. There is other energy, though: the metaphysical kind that can be manipulated and adapted to help you help yourself and others. It can sway you to finish projects and stop self-sabotaging and even persuade others. And, yes, it connects you to all living things, and these associations bring benefits. This energy connects us to our spiritual realm, filled with the messengers that bring you metaphysical knowledge. We need only be open enough to receive it and learn to interpret it.

We don't always recognize or understand our intuitive nudges. That's okay. Intuition will continue coming through any way it can, often using symbols to represent things that are familiar to you. To further your intuitive wisdom, you can create your own symbols journal to give you ongoing access to interpreting psychic messages. If you're still unaware of the extrasensory messages that are coming to you, go take a nap, literally. Your intuition often comes through in dreams and sometimes, unfortunately, as nightmares. Your subconscious provides an opening for symbolic messages, which may not be accessible while awake, to come in, though there are other ways to utilize your symbolic imagery during your conscious states as well.

During the cognizant moments, we recognize symbols through signs and synchronistic events. These are more tangible, easier ways to substantiate messages. Often, for people who have never experienced psychic phenomena, this will be their first introduction. This method seems to alleviate some of the doubt that it's imagination because they are external messages. Signs and synchronicities can be easier to recognize and seemingly less invasive when we are trying to tune in to situations or people, even if we have a hard time discerning the information otherwise. They can help validate our intuitive nudges.

We are all unique—we will all experience growth and the opportunity to see beyond our everyday existence in our own way, in our own time. But when we consciously acknowledge the universe sending us messages, we begin to let go of our self-imposed limitations. Instead, we broaden our scope of wisdom, and the challenges we face become alleviated. We have our superpower, our intuition, for illumination to light our way through self-discovery.

Part of that journey involves stepping out of our comfort zone and tapping into our intuition to heighten our judgment of which chances to take. Tuning in minimizes risks by removing fear of failure and instead increases your potential of success. Leveraging your intuition can influence your decision-making by giving you more information than you would have had with just your physical senses. Your intuitive vibes initiate a stronger platform for you to move forward in the right direction. But, of course, it's not just about you. It's also about how you work with others.

Tapping into others' energy, using your intuition, is one of the best ways to show people they and their opinions matter. But what do they want? What do your customers, bosses, spouses, peers, and even friends want from you? Sometimes, more importantly, how can you get them to want what you're selling? This presents you with a great opportunity to consider using your intuition. You need to draw out their desires by perceiving exactly what would make them want to spend their money, their time, and even their energy on what you have to offer. You have to make them feel like they *need* what you suggest. This is how marketing works: in essence, understanding what they want, often before they do, so you can give it to them and lead you *both* to success. When you market your stuff, it's essential they are interested. Tapping into what turns them on is the only way to make it a win-win situation.

First, though, land that job or that partner. Figuring out what the new prospective boss wants will give you a leg up over the other guy who is interviewing for the same position or contract. On the flip side, when you trust the vibes you are picking up off your employees, it makes it easier to understand where they are coming from and what will make them productive for you. And, remember, and I mean this in the best possible way, if you make them happy, you're happy. Plainly stated, tap into your intuition and you'll both be pleased.

It's easy to say using your intuition for yourself is a key component to being successful in business and life. But, to what extent should you use your intuition? *Go all in!* Celebrate your successes and even your failures—there is nothing better than learning from where you went wrong and stepping it up the next time to change the outcome. Nobody is ever 100 percent accurate when utilizing their natural intuitive gifts, but you will be 0 percent if you *never* use your innate abilities.

You need to practice using those gifts, and within these pages you'll have plenty of opportunities. Here's the thing about the exercises: these are only examples to use. They may or may not relate to you and your life. The circumstances are general and can be altered to fit what works for you. Feel free to adjust them so they make sense in your life. They are suggestions on how to access your gifts and will help you understand what type of method you can use in a particular situation to gain insight. Each person will resonate differently with each exercise as well as each type of intuitive ability. You'll discover this as you work your way through.

What it all comes down to is this: Do you want to be a badass in business and life? Do you want to be unapologetic for employing every faculty you can? Do you want to be successful in every area of your life? If you said yes, then you are ready to put your intuition to work.

# CHAPTER 1

# Demystifying Intuition in Business and Life

*Intuition is really a sudden immersion of the soul*
*into the universal current of life, where the histories*
*of all people are connected, and we are able to know*
*everything, because it's all written there.*

—PAULO COELHO, *THE ALCHEMIST*

There are so many unknowns in life and specifically in business. If it were super easy to succeed, everyone would. If the secrets were accessible, we'd all have the answers. What comes to mind when I tell you that you do indeed have the answers? Do you feel a bit of uneasy agitation because you doubt me? If you do, that's okay! You will learn how to protect yourself. When you are unfamiliar with your intuition, it can sometimes feel like some type of enchanted fairy tale, like it's something make-believe, and it can definitely feel unrealistic.

Let's take the *mystical* out of intuition if it makes you feel better. Let's, just for a second, pretend that it is a perfectly normal sense, as natural as your eyesight or your hearing or even your taste. I mean, how frequently do you feel comfortable talking to your coworkers about how you totally believe in intuition? It's probably not often you find yourself in the locker room discussing how you trusted your gut. You generally don't hear about how the presentation in the boardroom should be credited to intuitive inspiration. If you think of it as natural, instead of supernatural, it can change your world and become your superpower.

The fact is, in business and in most of life, we relate to things we can see or touch. We react to people, places, and things. In other words, we dig the tangibles—the concrete, perceptible stuff that is distinguishable from all the other stuff. It makes us feel comfortable. If we are able to define what that stuff is, it is much easier to tell ourselves it's real. It is quantifiable and we have evidence to prove it's clearly there, so we allow our brains to acknowledge it without question. The tangible things in life are easy to understand.

What's not quite as easy to believe in are the intangibles, things that we can't actually hold on to or touch. This is the stuff you must believe in almost solely on faith. Until, of course, you're able to wrap your mind around the fact that you don't always need to be able to touch something to believe that it's part of your reality.

## Superpower

Intuition is invisible. It is one of those tricky intangibles that you don't always understand. We can't reach out and touch it, and we don't always believe we have it. But our intuition *is* real. How do we know it's there if it's invisible? We can feel things, hear things, see things, smell things, and generally sense what is happening through our intuitive gifts. Intuition is that sixth sense, that extra metaphysical perceptive tool, that intangible gift, that amps up our five physical senses that we use to interpret information. Its preternatural almost, like things you only hear about with relation to the supernatural. Intuition really is our very own superpower, and we all have access to it every day.

Knowing you can have this as your superpower, what would you say about honing it? If you could have any superpower, what would it be? Would you have super sight? What about extraordinary hearing? How about being able to just know things? Or a supersensory feeling that tells you all about someone? These are all functions of our extrasensory capabilities. Let's explore them.

## The Clairs

*Clair* is the French word for "clear" and is used as a prefix to describe your different intuitive senses. We are all born with the ability to tap into them and utilize them every day. You might find, as you practice using them throughout the book, that you have a natural affinity toward one or two of these specific gifts. You will begin to appreciate which ones you are more connected with and which you feel strongest in. Through practice and repetition, you can cultivate and expand your innate gifts, though you might discover you won't quite connect to one or two of them, and that's normal. For example, similar to how not everyone will be a Mozart, not everyone will feel a kinship with their ability to hear psychic messages. Learning how to access each one of the clairs will uncover which you are more *and* less proficient with. So, let's dig in.

Let's break down the clairs and what they mean. Clairvoyance is clear psychic sight, being able to see things in your mind that aren't there in your physical reality. Clairaudience is psychic hearing, or the gift of hearing sounds or words or voices that aren't audible to the naked ear. Clairsentience is being able to feel things about others psychically, your gut instinct. And, a psychic knowing, or claircognizance, is when you know things that you have no reasonable basis for knowing. These psychic superpowers are available to you now, to help you in both business and everyday life. You will have multiple opportunities to begin tuning in to them all.

These are some of the most common psychic abilities. Do you immediately find yourself resonating with one or two of them? Does the mere mention of them bring back a memory of something for you? Whatever or however they make sense to you doesn't matter. That's right—it doesn't matter. What's more significant is that you become accustomed to the idea that these intuitive sensations are the real deal and that you are already benefitting from them. Whether it's a conscious or subconscious undertaking, it's happening regardless, so it's time you embrace it. Using your superpowers to gain impressions can be a driving force to get you to the next level of whatever you're trying to do.

Luckily, you aren't limited to having just one superpower. I mean, there are no superpower police to hold you back from that sweet flow of intuition, and there's no need to hide or ignore your gifts. It's time for you to lay it all on the table and show your hand. What do you see? What is there for you to leverage? You might find when you begin analyzing your intuitive gifts that you have more than you realize. Why not amp that up? Let's figure out which superpower you naturally have so you can, yes, use it to your advantage. If not, if you ignore it, you might fight your intuition will show up in a different way.

### Panic Attack

My friend Rebecca and her husband decided to put their house on the market. Unfortunately, shortly after that, her husband passed away from a quick bout with cancer. Rebecca wasn't sure what to do at that point, but she felt she had to continue looking for a new house. And then she found it. It seemed perfect. She loved it. It was a wonderful house that checked all the boxes for what she and her husband, Paul, had talked about before he died. She decided to put in an offer and planned on writing it up the next day.

During the process, she had a nagging feeling. She wasn't sure what it meant, so she pretty much ignored it. Was it just guilt that she was moving on? Was it because the house was over her budget? She didn't know and continued to dismiss the feeling until right before she was leaving to go put in an offer. She began experiencing heart palpitations, her body felt extremely stressed, and she broke out in a sweat. She was having a hard time breathing and felt very lightheaded. Immediately, she thought, "Oh my God. I'm having a heart attack."

Was she going to be joining Paul in the afterlife? Was it her time? What was going on? She took a breath, grabbed her phone, and, instead of calling her kids, decided quickly to look up the symptoms she was experiencing on her phone. She realized she was having a panic attack. Well, that was much better than a heart attack. This she could work with!

She realized in that moment that her intuition, along with her deceased husband, had been trying to tell her not to put an offer in for that house. She knew that was what the nagging feeling had been. She understood that it would be too far away from her kids, that she would be overextending herself, and that Paul was trying to say, "What the hell are you doing?"

Her intuition, her superpower, had been trying to let her know she needed to rethink her plan. She hadn't listened. In order to get her to stop and reevaluate, it caused her to have a full-blown panic attack, something she'd never had before. She knew without a doubt that the house was not supposed to be hers, and thank goodness she finally listened. Shortly after that, she ended up finding the perfect house, within her price range, with all the amenities she wanted. This house was within a mile of her son and within a mile of where her other son was working. It was the ideal spot for her to continue living. Paul was just going to have to wait for Rebecca to join him. Instead, she would live in her new home, happily trusting her intuition—and Paul—to continue leading her in the right direction.

As Rebecca discovered, your superpowers are there for a reason. They want to help you figure out what to do in life and business. As with Rebecca's story, if you ignore your intuition or don't pay attention to what your vibes are telling you, there can be consequences. If she hadn't had the panic attack, she would have been locked into a home she couldn't afford, away from her family, whom she much needed to be near, especially after Paul had passed, and she wouldn't have found her perfect place. A panic attack is a pretty extreme way of getting your attention—being aware of your intuitive gifts and heeding them is much better way to live! Rebecca discovered her superpower, which had kicked in via her intuitive feeling, or clairsentience. The question becomes, what is your superpower?

## Use That Vision: Clairvoyance

Are you the kind of person who sees only what they want to see? That won't work here. You need to be innovative as well as open to what your visions show you so you can be a success. Let go of your ego. Although at times it can provide you with protection or validation, it can also hold you back from trusting in the vision you need to succeed. Your ego can get in the way of being receptive to visual impressions because you might be blocking anything that doesn't come through to you via "normal" channels. The ego can keep you from truly seeing what you need to so that you can understand the messages you're getting. Dean Koontz, best-selling novelist, writes that "intuition is seeing with the soul."[4] We all have preconceived notions about what is real and what isn't, and if you don't grow up understanding that images you see in your mind can be something other than your imagination, it can make it difficult to believe they are real. Let's change that.

Using your intuition to see is actually very common, so common in fact that it has a name—*clairvoyance*—and no, it's not scary! Usually, we receive flashes or picturelike images in our mind, which can be hard to discern if you're not ready for them. Seeing these types of visions is not even something we readily acknowledge if we aren't used to it. However, as I already said, it is very common. Learning to interpret what we see plays a key role in understanding exactly what we are actually intuiting.

Believing what we see is equally important. Knowing there is a possibility that we are viewing images in our mind that are not just our imagination trying to play tricks can be a tough pill to swallow, but it's time! Don't ignore what can be potentially one of your greatest advantages in your business world. It's not always about not believing, though you have to learn to trust the difference between what is your imagination and what is your intuition. This comes with time and practice. Clairvoyance usually comes with a feeling. This helps you differentiate between your intuitive sight and your imagination.

## Try This!
## Visualize to Sell

How, you might ask, can clairvoyance help me in business? Let's pretend we have a product we need to market—the thingamabob. What do you want it to be? It can be anything your heart desires, or it can be something you are actively thinking of creating. Don't worry for now about whether it's real or ready for production. Just imagine it has already gone through everything it needs to and now you only have one more choice to make: you need to decide what color would boost

---

4. Dean Koontz, *The Darkest Evening of the Year* (New York: Bantam Dell, 2008), 429.

its marketability while appealing to the customers and possibly your client. Maybe you have already narrowed it down to three different colors; let's say blue, yellow, and red.

Now, visualize the thingamabob. Where would it be? Would it be on a shelf somewhere? Would it be online? Would it be in your customer's hands? At a boutique? Or a salon? Or a big-box store?

This is the cool part. See the product in its packaging—really look at it in your mind's eye. Trust the first image that comes to you. What do you see as the predominant color? When you see it now in your mind's eye, what color is it? Is it one of the three colors you were already thinking? Or something different? The thingamabob is now the perfect color, because you saw it clairvoyantly with your intuitive vision! This intuitive vision, clairvoyant sight, is there for you to take advantage of. Use it as you will. Discard any doubt you may have about whether or not this ability is available to you. Believe that you can envision things and you will start doing exactly that.

Using this example, you can also tune your vision in to what colors would absolutely not work, what packages would remain stuck on the shelf in retail hell, never making you or your customers any money. Because we are in it to win it, we want to use that sight any way we can to help make us successful. After all, it's part of your birthright, so why not discover how your vision can easily be enhanced to increase your success?

### Visualize Your Goals

Your third eye, your psychic sight, can be used to help you get ahead in business. It is a powerful, innate tool you can utilize. It's actually a prevalent sense for people who are more visual, like artists or photographers. Utilizing this gift can help you solve problems, get answers, and possibly even get advanced comprehension of what's to come.

So often people discount the visions they see in their mind's eye because they feel like it's merely wishful thinking that they are seeing something positive, or they feel like what they are perceiving is not a true intuitive vision but that they are seeing something born of fear. When we are afraid something is not right, our imagination can come up with the craziest notions, which often show up masquerading as intuitive images. This may lead to confusion and at times create doubt. Practicing using your intuition undoubtedly will relieve some of the bewilderment.

Think of your third eye as an extension of you. It is one of your natural senses, though grossly undervalued. Having access to this can give you clarity when you need direction. Suppose you are a waiter and you have a decent job. Imagine someone comes into your place of employment and tells you they know of a great opportunity where you could make double the tips with less work. They tell you they just opened a new restaurant and they think you'd be perfect there. They give you their business card and ask you to let them know. You finish your shift, all the while weighing your pros and cons of leaving where you currently are versus this great new restaurant. So far, it's a fifty-fifty split. How can you decide? This is where your intuitive vision comes in.

You've exhausted all logical debates, so now it's time to see what the outcome would be with your mind's eye. If you ask to see the answer to "Should I stay or should I go?" the universe will respond. It may not happen instantly, but usually you'll get some type of response shortly after. Let's say an hour later you see a red hexagon shape in what you think may be your imagination, but you're not entirely sure what it means. The cool thing is you can ask for clarification. When you do, you see a stop sign. This is a symbolic message that your intuition is giving to you to make it easier to recognize your sixth sense. You can be reasonably assured it is a directive to not make the move.

Let's pretend you're still curious and want to know why you shouldn't take the proffered job. You can ask for another vision, possibly a precognitive sight that will show you the future. If you draw all your attention to the center of your forehead, you can kind of jump-start your gifts. Envisioning a blank piece of photo paper, you could ask for an image to show you what would happen if you were to take the new position. At first, the paper may look blank, but give it a chance. Soon enough, that paper may start to fill in, showing you pictures in your mind's eye of what would have been. These images, along with the original stop sign vision, are enough to help you understand that by not accepting the job, you are making a better decision.

## Try This!
## How to Visualize Your Goals

This intuitive vision is also where you can conceptualize your goals. Then, by setting your intention, you can use your clairvoyance to help you realize your goals. Ask questions such as the following and expect to see your answers. Again, they may not happen instantly, so give them time!

- Is my goal going to be beneficial to me?
- Am I headed in the right direction to achieve my goal?
- What steps should I take to reach my goal?
- Does it make sense to go after this?
- Will I be able to realize my goal within a month? A year? Five years?
- Is there anything I should be on the lookout for?
- Is there anything I should avoid?
- Should I adjust my goal?

Asking these questions, along with any others you can think of, can help you accomplish what you set out to do. You are planting the visual seeds by expecting answers. Now all that's left to do is to follow the images your clairvoyance is showing you and you'll be on your way to attaining your goal.

There are no rules when it comes to your clair senses. Using your vision to support your business endeavors will give you so much more insight than just utilizing data or even guessing in order to make decisions. Using your other intuitive gifts will increase your advantages even more. You will absolutely benefit by tapping into and even combining your other senses as well. Think of your abilities as a metaphysical garden, ripe and ready to be picked.

# That Inner Voice: Clairaudience

We've all heard it—that inner voice that talks to us even when we don't want it to. Sometimes it's a quiet, gentle voice and sometimes, it's loud and nagging and won't leave you alone. That's your intuitive guidance, your inner counsel, trying to help you. When the nagging voice escalates, it's usually because you're not listening, kind of like when you didn't listen to your mom or your partner. It's saying, "Pay attention to what I'm telling you! I am trying to help you!"

In business, we have that same voice, waiting to be heard, trying to provide direction to us. It goes beyond balance sheets and bottom lines. It is that first, and what should be the last, directive we have. Depending on tactical and strategic data alone to provide us with definitive guidance is extremely limiting. Intuition is a powerful business tool and we would be foolish to overlook it. We have the option to employ so many techniques. We would be remiss to restrict ourselves and not use everything in our arsenal. The more we listen to our inner voice, the stronger it gets and the easier it will get to rely on its accuracy, which ultimately can increase our bottom line.

Do you enjoy listening to music? Talking to people? If so, this may indicate that you have a natural *clairaudient* slant to your intuitive awareness. This means that you may be more inclined to hear the information that will help you flourish in business and life. Unlike clairvoyance, this intuitive hearing will present itself audibly, rather than visually. And, no, hearing voices does not necessarily mean you're crazy! Rather, it might instead prove to you that you can indeed gain valuable assistance.

So how do you tune in to your psychic hearing? Start by listening. *Be quiet!* Are you the one who doesn't know how to shut the heck up? Do you find yourself talking over others or constantly telling others your stories without hearing theirs? Listen, I get it. When I get passionate about a subject or have (at least what I think is) a great tale to tell, I tend to ramble on as well. But in order to really tune in and allow your intuition to come through so you can hear it, you need to pipe down. Revel in the serenity of the quietness around you for a moment. You can't hear anything if you are constantly making noise.

Now that you've quieted down, what can your extrasensory hearing tell you? It depends what answers you need. Anything you can have answered in the physical world can also be answered metaphysically. Stop for a minute and pretend that you want some business guidance. The problem is you don't have anyone around you that you can ask for help, so you need to get your answers yourself. Perfect! This is where your clairaudience comes in.

### Try This!
### Listen Up

What kind of direction are you looking for? Much the same as we did with our clairvoyance, we can ask anything we want in this clairaudience exercise. How about we start with something good? Using your imagination, you can imitate how it can work for you by making a mental list of questions, and then ask them out loud or just in your mind and wait for an answer. One of the easiest ways to do this is to think of yes-or-no questions as they pertain to your subject. For the sake of practicing your gifts, I'm going to give you a few sample questions:

- Should I look for a new job?
- Would I be happier doing something else?
- Would I make more money if I switched positions?
- Do I already know what career would be ideal for me?
- Even though I'm not making a lot now, should I stick with it?
- Should I ask for a promotion?
- Should I ask for a raise?
- Should I start my own business?
- Would I make more money on my own?
- Should I pitch this new product or plan to my boss or customer?
- Is it time to create something new?
- Should I fire my employee?
- Should I move my business or home?

While all these questions may not be specific for you, you can cater them and ask whatever you want. But wait for an answer. Remember, you want to ask yes-or-no questions. Be Zen-like. Quiet. Peaceful. And expect to hear a response. It might take you a bit of time to hear it but give it a good three to four minutes before moving on to your next question. You can always go back to it. You might not hear a yes or no. Lisa K., PhD, author and teacher, agrees that "when you first ask your intuition a question, especially when you are first learning, you probably won't understand what the answer means. If you don't understand the message you can ask again, and ask for clarity."[5] You might instead get something that means yes or no, such as "sure" or "okay" for yes or "not" or "veto" for no. If you receive an answer but can't tell if it is a yes or a no because it is revealing itself in an imprecise way, ask for clarity. This is about you, so take advantage of it and listen!

### Listening with Your Intuition

Some people find it difficult to drown out the noise, specifically the background static. It reminds me of a commercial I used to see on television that advertised a hearing aid to get rid of the sounds that weren't important so you could hear the ones that were. This to me is what really needs to be done in order to successfully use your clairaudience.

John, a client of mine, came in for a session one day. He described to me how he had been trying to tap into his intuition but was having a very difficult time. He needed to decide whether or not to sell his company, and having previously trusted his intuition in other business matters, he was quite disappointed that he wasn't able to tune in this time.

"I am hoping you can get a feel for what I should do. I can't seem to get a line on it," he told me.

"I can definitely give it a shot!" I told him.

---

5. Lisa K., *Intuition on Demand: A Step-By-Step Guide to Powerful Intuition You Can Trust* (Scotland: Findhorn Press, 2017), 32.

"Good, because it seems like I have a million voices and sounds coming at me all at once. I can't decipher anything. I don't even know if I'm actually getting any messages or not because I can't sift through the noise," he explained further.

"Well, let's see what we get," I responded.

I began tuning in, opening up all my senses to receive whatever I could. I expected to utilize most of my gifts as that is my norm, but I was surprised to get the same type of response as John.

"I hear some chatter," I told him. "It seems really loud. I am going to work on trying to weed out what is important."

I opened up my clairaudient senses further, rather than trying to shut down the noise. Then, I cleared my mind, grounded myself down to the earth, and opened myself up to the energy so I could raise my vibration. By quieting my spirit, I was able to tap into the universal energy. Remaining in this meditative state for a bit, I asked the universe to help me. What I began to decipher made me stop and laugh.

"I totally get what you're talking about! It sounds like I'm in the middle of a dance club!"

But what was even more significant was the song I started to make out amidst all of the hullabaloo.

"I think you should definitely sell. First of all, I hear what sounds like people laughing and dancing and celebrating. But, even more significantly, I'm hearing the song 'I Feel Good,' which tells me that you for sure should do it. The exhilaration will last for a long time!"

Sometimes the noise you hear is actually part of the message. Listening to everything can be difficult when you are trying to listen to your clairaudient senses, which is what happened to John. He was getting his answer but just having trouble interpreting it. There are no precise directions when trying to weed through what you're hearing. Raising your vibration can help you sort out the noise, to either interpret all that you're hearing or quiet down what is not significant. Overall, using your clairaudience, and all your intuitive abilities, further strengthens your power in a world where you should take advantage of all the opportunities you can to succeed. Learning to ground yourself is an essential part of that, regardless of which clair sense you are using.

*Try This!*
## Ground Yourself to Raise Your Vibration

Be somewhere comfortable and quiet. Close your eyes and take a deep breath. When you're ready, imagine that coming out of the bottom of your feet are roots. These roots are reaching deep down into the ground. They continue reaching all the way down to a giant boulder in the center of the earth and wrap themselves around it.

Now, as you continue breathing deeply, imagine there is positive earth energy rising up through the roots into the soles of your feet. As it rises up, you can feel it warming your feet, your ankles, and your calves, all the way up to your knees. Feel that energy moving up even further, and as it does, it is clearing out any psychic debris that no longer belongs there.

Feel the energy continuing up through your thighs, into your hips and your abdomen, getting rid of any negativity you don't need to hold on to. Allow it to move up even more, into your chest area, warming your body and clearing anything that is no longer yours.

The warm earth energy now moves into your neck and shoulders, relieving any tension you may have, and continues into your face and your head. As it does, it removes any lingering stress in your jaw and your forehead.

Now the beautiful earth energy moves to the top of your head, where there is a funnel opening up toward the heavens. As it does, feel it rising, almost stretching you up, pulling your energy strongly but calmly through the tunnel. Your incredible earth energy is mixing now, with the energy of the universe, and as it does your vibration is lifted, flowing toward the vibration of the universe, mixing and melding together. You may even find you feel lighter as your vibration is raised.

When you are ready, take a deep breath and open your eyes. You've raised your vibration, which can help you connect on a deeper level. It can also aid with opening up your ability to interpret and translate intuitive messages. Whether using your clairaudience or any other clair sense, you can always stop, take a deep breath, ground yourself, and raise your vibration to allow you to better connect.

Listening with your clairaudience is an important tool. Learning how to listen in any situation is important, but going deeper with your intuition gives you a stronger connection to people in general. If you are having a conversation, listen to what's not being said—employ your gifts to gain a deeper understanding of what is significant to the person you're talking to. For example, if they say one thing to you, but you hear something else, pay attention. It may be the universe sending you a message. If while they're talking about opening a new business, you hear the ominous sounds of the beginning of Beethoven's Fifth Symphony, it might help them to let them know to be sure they've researched everything about their prospective endeavor. If they ask why, tell them the truth—I heard it! It's their choice whether they heed your advice and use it to their benefit. Your clairaudience may just help them be more successful.

## Getting the Feels: Clairsentience

We all know we get in our feels sometimes. Simply put, we can feel things deeply, and this in turn can change how we act or react to things. They can also adjust, almost automatically, what we choose to do. Well, similar to our emotional feelings, our intuitive feelings are just as valuable in swaying our opinions. Called *clairsentience,* these psychic impressions can give us goosebumps and cause us to question what the heck is happening. These goosebumps are nothing to mess around with! They are your body manifesting proof that your sensory input is alive and well.

Clear intuitive feelings contribute to decision-making. These (sometimes gentle) nudges can really sway your opinions about everything from evaluating a new project at work to which comforter your daughter would like for her college dorm room. It's the trusting of this mostly subtle vibe that can be difficult. Listen, I know it would be easier if your gut instincts could be clearer, but would you want your stomach clenching up uncontrollably every single time you felt something negative? Or would you rather it be a bit more restrained? Once you learn to recognize them, your psychic feelings will give you a huge advantage.

Now that you know about your extrasensory feelings, how do you actually recognize your clairsentience as being more than just indigestion? You practice. You won't always readily understand your metaphysical feelings or what they are telling you, but the more you work with this ability, the stronger it will become. You will begin to recognize how it feels in your body. You may get goosebumps or a tingly feeling or even butterflies in your belly, and these are all validation that your senses are working.

Think about when you walk into a room and the tension is so thick you can cut it with a knife. You're not picking up on that because of the décor or what is being served. Nope. It's about the energy of the people. Even if outwardly they show no signs of having been arguing or angry, you can feel it. That's your clairsentience, and damn if it doesn't affect you too, especially if you are empathic, meaning you feel what others feel. This enhances your clairsentience tenfold and can wreak havoc if you don't protect yourself.

Envision yourself walking into a work meeting. You've gotten there a bit late because you had to put together a presentation. You skip through the doorway, excited about the brilliant idea you are going to share with them, only to feel like you are hit in the gut. It can stop you dead in your tracks and change your entire mindset. That's because you feel the people already in the room have a negative attitude in some way. They've been arguing, or maybe it's as simple as they just don't feel like being there. Maybe they are a bit jealous that you were given this opportunity that they wanted. It doesn't even matter what it is, just that you can feel it and there's no way in hell you think you can get back the enthusiasm you felt seconds before.

So what can you do now? You adjust. You know that you've picked up on the less-than-positive energy, so immediately you can adapt and redirect your own energy to pick up the pieces you've been left with. If you had no connection to your clairsentience, you would not be able to quickly adjust, but because you are an intuitive badass, you can! You know from the vibes that the energy you walked into has nothing to do with you, so you don't have to doubt yourself. This automatically gives you a leg up toward your own personal success.

One of the best ways to tune in to your intuition is to pay attention to how your body feels. When you are trying to decide on something for business, notice if your body feels good or bad. When you are thinking of your situation, become aware of whether your body feels heavy or light. Also, does it make you feel happy? Mad? Sick? Excited? All these intuitive feelings can be good indicators of your clairsentience providing you with answers.

## Try This!
## Get in Your Feels

You can take this as far as you'd like, but you should start with the basics. Practice feeling with your gut instincts by tuning in about certain situations in your life. Pay attention to your body's initial response to the following situations or people; you want to go with your first impression, which is usually the most accurate with clairsentience. Notice, for each one, if you have overall positive or negative feelings and more specifically if they make you feel happy or angry or even ill or ramped up. These are the cues that your clairsentient gifts are kicking in.

- Your current job
- Your significant other
- Your family
- Your career path in general
- Your health
- Your boss
- Your employee

- Your home
- Furthering your education or training
- Your financial balance

After you've given yourself a bit of time to really experience how each item made you feel, you can weed out the negative ones and start making plans to change those aspects in your life. By utilizing your clairsentience, you have quickly gained access to what your intuition is telling you, without question. Now, it's up to you to get the ball rolling in your favor!

## What You Know: Claircognizance

Does it ever seem like a lamp just switched on in your head? Like the light bulb didn't just flicker but really lit up. So often it's your *claircognizance*, or your clear knowing, that surprises you—it's your extrasensory perception that occurs when you just know something, even though you really have absolutely no actual basis for the knowledge. But you all of a sudden know it, without a doubt. It's like a vent just opened and the understanding just floated in out of nowhere.

This gift is actually more common than you may be aware of. Though similar to clairsentience or clear feeling, claircognizance is more black and white, more definitive. Imagine needing to decide if you should invest in a particular market or stock. If you use your intuitive feeling sense, it might leave you a little wishy-washy, and that is no place to be when you want to spend your hard-earned cash. Tapping into your clear knowing, however, can tell you yes or no, good or bad, and give you a very conclusive answer.

This knowing can come through in many ways, and however it works for you doesn't matter. Usually, it's a combination of gifts that impresses the knowing upon you. For example, you might be looking at two different business prospectuses, and all of a sudden you just know you should invest in business A over business B because you're drawn to it and it's like you saw a beam of light highlighting it. Regardless of how the initial knowing happens, you usually have some type of supporting intuitive guidance to confirm it.

What's interesting about this type of impression is that it can be harder to trust than your other intuitive senses. The others can provide you with a kind of backup, like even though you can't see anything with your physical eyes, clairvoyance offers you images in your mind's eye. With this mode of perception, you must rely on and be confident in your own gifts. Otherwise, you will doubt yourself every time, and that can really suck. Learning to have faith in your ability to discern using your claircognizance will eventually lead you to expect that it will happen and help you when you need it.

As if you don't have enough to think about, we're going to add some more. You can count on your instincts to just seemingly randomly show up with answers to things you didn't even know you had questions about! Yes, this really happens. Take a moment to wrap your head around it. For the sake of practicing, we can work with a variety of subjects but leave the timeline a bit loose. Here are a couple of topics to let marinate in your mind throughout the day. Just allow yourself to receive a response. When you know the answer, you'll just know. Don't question it. Just believe it. And more importantly, don't think about the question after you ask it. You can read these aloud or in your mind, whichever you prefer.

- When's the next job coming?
- What can I do to get my name out there more?
- How should I pursue a collaboration for a new partnership?
- What can I do to make a lot of money over the next month?
- How can I leverage my intuition every day?
- Where would be most beneficial for me to live?
- What franchise would best suit me?
- Where should I take my team on a retreat?
- What type of retreat should I lead?
- What should I pitch my boss?
- What flavors would my customers consider best for my newest item?

Again, feel free to tailor your questions to your life and your work. The most important thing here is to be open—expect an answer to just sort of show up over the course of the next day or two. Your knowing may come in conjunction with your other intuitive senses or just as the light bulb–like spark of understanding. It might appear in an image or with a sound or even a feeling, but it will be a very distinctive realization of what your inner guidance is telling you. Pay attention! This may be the only guidance you get, and it can make or break your decisions.

The knowing can show up when you least expect it. In high school my husband was secretly in love with me, although we didn't even officially meet until my twenties. At that point, I was not interested in anything more than a friendship. I had recently gotten out of an intense relationship and quite frankly wanted my freedom. This time, he was not taking no for an answer, and he not only talked to me but continually asked me out in a friendly, I-am-totally-into-you way. However, I kept saying no—I just wanted to be friends. Until that one day.

That day, so long ago, I was at the beach with my girlfriend watching a softball game. He and I had had a lengthy conversation about a week prior about how much I liked riding motorcycles, and he explained he'd ridden since he was a little kid. He told me he was thinking of buying a new bike. Well, he did, and he showed up at the beach, asking if I wanted to take a ride with him in a bit. I said okay but wanted to wait until the game was over. When he came back, I got on the back of the bike, which in and of itself is rare because I don't usually trust other riders, and I put my arms around him. The second I did, I felt like I was home. That was it. No other way to describe it. I just knew we were meant to be together. I knew it, though I hadn't felt that way with him at all, even after all his attempts at getting me to date him. Two weeks later he moved in, and we've been happily married for over twenty years. I felt his energy attached to mine, and it just felt complete.

I understood in that moment that my intuition was telling me something very important. He apparently knew since high school; it just took me a while to catch up. I share this story not as a means for you to find your next significant other, though it can definitely help you, but as an example of how incredibly powerful your intuitive awareness can be when you're not even trying. Think of what I would have missed out on had I not been open to my claircognizance. Imagine how mighty it can be when you focus on it.

## Employing All Your Gifts

All your intuitive gifts can be employed individually and in conjunction with the others. Knowing which one you are utilizing is not as important as simply using them. Frequently, it can be hard to decipher which ability is giving you the guidance you're looking for, as they may actually blend together. Remember the basics, though. Clairvoyance is about seeing an image in your mind's eye and can be used when looking for an answer symbolic in nature. You can also rely on the snapshot-like images it will present to you. Clairaudience provides you with auditory insight and can be helpful when you are trying to understand a name or even when you need directions on how to accomplish something. Clairsentience helps you feel things with your gut instincts and can help you gauge a situation. Claircognizance is there to give a no-nonsense answer or to allow you to instantly know and understand a situation. Having said this, you are not limited to using one ability over another for anything. The examples listed here are just common functions and a brief introduction so you can practice.

By now the concept of and using your intuition may be second nature. You've probably discovered one or two psychic senses you can relate to naturally. We come into this world with intuitive gifts, and now that they've been demystified, it should be even easier to tune in to them. According to Rick Snyder, business intuitive, "Intuition is connected to a deeper intelligence inside all of us that enriches our lives personally, professionally, and creatively."[6]

You have all the clair tools you need to really start tuning in. Both your waking moments and your dreamscape contain flashes of intuitive awareness. You may have found yourself feeling more successful with one or two of the earlier exercises—this may suggest you are stronger in that particular ability. Did you figure out if you possess predominately one sense or another?

6. Rick Snyder, *Decisive Intuition: Use Your Gut Instincts to Make Smart Business Decisions* (Newburyport, MA: Career Press, 2019), 8.

All these gifts can help you with your life changes and can vary from situation to situation. Just when you think you know exactly how you tap into your vibes, you may realize you are getting your impressions differently, so you really must step it up and always be alert. Although you might discover that you just don't click with a specific gift initially, you possibly get better at developing it the more you practice using it. You also may realize that all of a sudden that same gift just pops up to help you. You become more aware of each of your gifts as you utilize them, and depending on the circumstances, you can really count on your intuition to help you on your path to being fiercely successful, especially when you protect yourself.

## Stay Protected

You've learned what it means to tune in, but do you know how to protect yourself when you do? Essentially, you need to protect your energy so you don't get attacked or take on the energy of other people. Think back to walking into that room full of negativity. What you feel can be absorbed if you're not careful. Whether you have a natural empathic propensity or not doesn't matter—what does matter is that psychic vampires (people who feed off others emotionally and psychically) are everywhere, and they can suck your energy dry without even meaning to.

Before employing your intuitive gifts in your professional or personal life, you should create a circle of protection around yourself. This is one of the easiest and quickest ways to ensure your energy stays unharmed and positive. Imagination and visualization, which you've just developed, are the main facilities you need to safeguard yourself.

### *Try This!*
### Create Your Own Bubble

For your first time you'll want privacy. You'll also want to be somewhere you can relax and sit or lie comfortably. When you are ready, close your eyes and take a deep breath. Then another. When you breathe in again, imagine a beautiful silver bubble beginning to grow, starting at the bottom of your feet. Imagine on the next inhalation that bubble growing, moving up around your knees and your hips, moving around your torso. Take another deep breath and visualize that bubble spreading all the way up around your neck and your arms and to the top of your head.

This bubble allows the oxygen you need to come in, but it keeps any negativity out. Visualize this bubble continuing to grow, expanding out four feet from you, shimmery and silver. As your bubble gets bigger, set your intention to only allow positivity to flow in and to protect you from anyone who tries to suck energy from you. Continuing to breathe, visualize your bubble of protection and know that it can be created anytime you need to work with your intuitive gifts to keep you safe from anyone else's energy or negativity. Relax and revel in your protected space for another moment or two. When you're ready, open your eyes, leaving your bubble around you.

You've not only protected yourself, but you have made your intuitive abilities, the clairs, accessible. You've essentially got your gifts with you at all times, in your pockets. You'll have plenty of time to apply your newly opened abilities throughout the rest of these pages. As you move forward, you'll want to know where those vibes come from, and you'll need to understand how to receive and interpret the impressions simply and in a way that makes sense for you.

# CHAPTER 2
# Our Helpers and Tools

*It seems to be not so much a matter of whether or not we are intuitive, but where and how our intuition comes forth in our lives.*

—SHERRIE DILLARD, *DISCOVER YOUR PSYCHIC TYPE*

Using your intuition may not feel familiar to you. That's okay. In fact, it's quite normal. When you do something you're not accustomed to doing, it can feel foreign, like it doesn't quite fit. Until it does. You will become more comfortable with it, as you would anything, as you put more effort into using it. For example, you use your eyes to see and your ears to hear, physically, without questioning that ability because it is part of your everyday normalcy. It is fascinating to think using our metaphysical sight and hearing can be just as consistent. Your curiosity, by now, should be piqued. The prospect of thriving in business can drive your growth and accelerate your desire to develop your gifts even more.

When we begin shifting our awareness to align our soul or our spirt with our physical and mental self, we grow exponentially. When you live with a more self-centered viewpoint, it tends to feel like you have to do everything by yourself. Alternatively, it's easier when you have someone you trust to help you expand your awareness. When opening your extrasensory perception, you are also unlocking your connection to your psychic helpers, the ones you'll learn have your back at all times. And these helpers have developed a symbolic language to communicate with you in the most efficient way possible.

On a basic level, we gain access to these messages with our clair senses, but sometimes we could use a little more assistance with perceiving them. This is where intuitive tools come in. These are aids we can use to support our intuition. Tools make it easier to comprehend information when you need an answer quickly or when you need validation that what you've intuited is right. Although it is not essential that you use them, you might experience a jump-start in discerning the messages from your helpers when you do.

## Your Helpers

If you're curious like me, now that you've been introduced to your gifts, you may want to know where they come from or, more specifically, where the information is coming from. Before you can begin truly using your gifts, you should understand what they are and how they are delivered to you. Now, this may be a somewhat strange concept, but your intuition is there because you have a connection to the universe, to everything in the world. That said, you are able to tap into the energy of the universe in order to receive messages intuitively. These messages will come in a variety of ways, from your clairs and from a few different sources.

The most common form of intuition feels like it comes from inside, which can make it difficult to separate from your imagination. That sense you get comes from a source that connects to you through what Carl Jung referred to as the collective unconscious, that connection we share. It's a vibe you get, a feeling, a flash, and when it's your intuition talking to you, it feels a bit different from your imagination, possibly more stimulating. It may even cause you to have an emotional or visceral reaction. The messages tend to feel a bit more charged with energy, less flat. It can come across as a kind of rush and lift you up. The messages you may receive are from your spirit guides, your angels, and even your deceased loved ones.

These messengers will use any method they can to help you utilize your intuition through your psychic senses by sending you data you can interpret within your psyche. While we're not going to put too much focus on your helpers, it is good to know where your information is coming from so you can be confident it is coming from a positive source.

## Spirit Guides

Your spirit guides are with you at all times. They are there in the background, providing you with those aha moments, those times when it feels like your intuition just clicks. They are around you to provide you with everything you need to lead a fulfilled life. Spirit guides most likely were not alive when you were born but have at one time, probably way back, walked the earth and are now here to help you. They are evolved spirits and have a direct line into your life and know what course is best for you to reach your greatest potential.

Spirit guides try to guide you with love and positive direction, though we so often don't listen. For example, it's difficult to succumb to letting go of something we want, even if it is not for our greater good. We tend to push the envelope and complain when something doesn't work out the way we want it to. What we may not be aware of is our guides have been there, holding our hands, trying to lead us in a better, more beneficial direction, but we haven't recognized it. We've been too busy swimming upstream, against the current, to notice their sometimes subtle, yet always present guidance.

When we try to control everything, alone, without checking in with them, we can become frustrated. It can feel like we have to accomplish everything by ourselves and the struggle is real. When we take a step back and ask our guides to help show us the right path, we find that what we want may not be on that route and we will be better off shifting and changing our trajectory a bit. Our spirit guides assist us in creating confidence and strength, providing us with counsel to help us be successful.

These psychic helpers are working hard to expose pitfalls as well as advantages along our journey. In business, they try to lead you to make the best choices to manage your career. They oversee your actual occupation and inspire you to be the best version of you that you can be. They encourage you to shift and change course toward positive outcomes but will also hang back and let you learn lessons when you're not paying attention. They want to let you know they are with you and work tirelessly to break down the boundaries and barriers you've put between you by ignoring their messages. The more you learn to discern their guidance, the more you'll recognize when they are trying to communicate. Above all, they want to help you succeed, which you will notice as your perception grows stronger.

### *Try This!*
### Meet Your Spirit Guide

Though it is not always necessary to know who your guides are, it often brings comfort to put a name or even a face to those who are working so hard on our behalf. To honor your guides and make them, in your mind, more accessible, let's meet them. Go somewhere you can lie down or sit comfortably. Start by closing your eyes and breathe deeply. Continue this until you are totally relaxed.

Then, using your imagination, see yourself in a beautiful green meadow, filled with blossoms of all colors. To the left, there are purple flowers and yellow flowers in full bloom. To your right you can see amazing red and blue flowers and in front of you a radiant bright orange and yellow sun. The sun is shining down, the perfect temperature for you, illuminating a pathway made of soft stone.

As you follow the pathway, you come to a bright white bench. The bench is wooden and is covered by a pergola. Climbing the pergola are pulsating, healing green vines, with blossoming purple flowers. It creates a safe and protective covering while letting the restorative sun rays shine through. Sit down on the bench, knowing you are sheltered from any negative energy.

Next ask for your spirit guide to come and join you on the bench. Watch as they walk toward you. Notice what they look like. Do they have clothes on? If so, what color are they? Do they have hair or something else on their head? Can you see their features? Notice their eye color. What does their gender appear to be? Make room for them to join you on the bench.

Now, ask them their name. Ask for them to tell you clearly so you can understand it. If you don't get a response or can't decipher it, ask them again. If you still don't hear their answer, ask them to write it in the dirt in front of you. Watch as they spell it out. If you still don't hear it or see it, pay attention to whether you feel it. You may just know what their name is instantly. If you still aren't getting a name, that's okay. Just relax and know it will come to you when it needs to.

Then, ask them if they have a gift for you. They have brought you something and it will help you on your journey—if you are focused on business, it may be something to help you move up or to guide you toward a new career. If you are focusing on your personal life, it might be a present to help you heal in some way. If it is wrapped or in a box or covered by something, go ahead and open it. Look at it. Do you know what it is? Does it feel heavy or light in your hands? What color is it? What does it mean to you? Does it make sense? Does it help provide you with an answer to a question you may have? Whatever it is, accept it and receive it with love because that is how they are giving it to you.

Finally, ask them if there is anything else they need to tell you. Receive their words of wisdom. Then thank them. Take a few deep breaths, and when you are ready, open your eyes.

Were you able to see them? Hear them? Feel them? Did you receive a gift? Words of wisdom? Did it feel natural or forced? Did it make you happy?

Your spirit guides are around for you to ask them for guidance. After you have met them, it is sometimes easier to ask for their help by having someone to focus your energy on—you probably, now, know their name and what they look like, which can give you a greater sense of connection to your intuition.

These guides are your most helpful daily form of assistance, and they're there to offer practical support. You've also got angels. They are around for the really big, lifesaving type of events. These are the ones you've heard of that help a mother lift a car off her child after an accident. They are responsible for these types of events, and although they are around when you need them, they are not like the spirit guides. They are not there for the little things, the everyday details in business or life, as your guides are.

Often confused with spirit guides, angels are messengers from another realm. They have never walked the earth. However, you can always call them in when you need help, especially if you feel you are at the end of your rope. Your spirit guides, though, are the ones you'll want to work with to increase your business. They are the ones who will help you expand overall.

## Deceased Loved Ones

You have loved ones on the other side. They, like you, have been in human form and understand the pressures of real life. They have made choices and reaped the benefits and the consequences while they were alive. They are around to share their love with you.

Your deceased loved ones can help you, but they can only help you with things they understood or knew in life. For example, if you have a best friend who was terrible at business but incredible at dancing, you wouldn't call for their wisdom when you are trying to close a big business deal, unless that deal had something to do with dance. My mom was an amazing nurse but always struggled with finances. I always ask her for her healing and protective energy. However, I would not ask for her help with money issues.

Your friends and family come through to send you love. They want to let you know they are still around. They are there to share the magical moments in your life and retain much of the same traits and personalities they had when they were alive. They want you to be happy and will show up to wish you well.

All your helpers are there for you. They will send you messages to help you or just to say hello. It can be difficult for us to receive the messages, especially when we are new to working with our intuition. But our guides and helpers want you to understand, so they will use the easiest method they can to get through to you. They will use symbols that you can recognize so their messages will make sense.

## Symbols

Learning to interpret psychic messages can be confusing. Even when employing all our clair senses, there is still a level of discernment needed. Psychic symbols are a language much like any other; however, they have one major difference—they are customized for you. Psychic language needs to be developed and created for each individual. To understand this symbolic communication, we have to personalize it. While there are many common and universal symbols, such as a stop sign, for example, there are just as many, if not more, that are unique. This is because we each have our own distinctive lives, and it is through the memories and our recall of things that our symbols are fashioned.

Peter came in for a reading. He was concerned about his business: "I am not sure whether to sell my business or keep it. I really want to be able to pass it down to my children, but I am so divided over whether that would be a worthwhile endeavor."

I tuned in to his energy and the energy of his company. What I saw immediately seemed pretty clear.

"Are you a landscaper or something? I'm seeing a field of grass with a lawn mower sitting right smack dab in the middle," I told him.

"Yes, I am. I created my company from scratch, and it's pretty decent now. I have a few employees and we are always busy, but I'm not sure if it's worth hanging on to it long term or not," he replied.

I focused on his business some more. More symbols were coming in, but these seemed a bit different. This time, I was seeing some of the cast from a television show. I couldn't quite understand it, so I told him.

"Okay, this is kind of strange, but I'm seeing Mike, Vinny, and Pauly from the show *Jersey Shore*. Does this mean anything to you?"

He started laughing and then answered, "It absolutely does. That's so funny! I never thought of that. My business is named MVP Landscape, and they always say 'MVP' on that show for the guys' initials!"

Okay, that *was* funny! I knew I was tapped in, but I needed to continue. I had to know whether it was worth it for him to keep the business in the hope his children, as they grew up, would take it over. I asked my guides to send me a symbol or something that would explain it further. What I got didn't seem to make sense to me, but I knew I had to share what I received, in the way I got it. It was not for me to interpret it. It was a message for Peter.

"What I am seeing is a little boy in diapers, holding hands with a toddler, and they both have really big sneakers on. I'm not sure what that symbolizes for you, but it's really cute!" I told him.

"Hah! Thanks so much! You've given me my answer. I'm excited now. I am going to keep my business," Peter told me, visibly excited.

"Let me in on it! What does it mean?" I knew it had to be significant in some way but I couldn't quite put it together.

"I never told anyone but my wife. I kept saying, the only reason I would keep the company together would be if my kids wanted to take over, if they wanted to fill my shoes when they got older. They are very young right now, a baby and a toddler! So what you said, about two young boys in big sneakers is extremely symbolic and means more than you can imagine," he exclaimed happily.

Turns out he really wanted to be able to pass down the business to his sons, but because they were so young, he had no idea if they'd want it. He'd received an offer to sell his landscape company, and he just wanted to be sure that turning it down would be the right move. What I saw meant nothing to me other than two cute kids. But when I told him what I'd seen, it meant the world. It was his symbol, personalized to his life.

Now, the funny thing is whenever this type of question comes up in a client reading, I will see those same kids. If they are wearing the huge sneakers, I know the business will last and be passed down. If they are barefoot, it's time to let it go and move on. Just because they aren't my kids and it wasn't initially my symbol doesn't negate what it now represents for me. This is how your personal symbolic language is developed.

Everyone's symbols will be different, though there will also be some similarities. For instance, if you are asking whether to get into business with someone and you see an image of a storm, chances are it will be a tumultuous relationship at best. If you are more auditory, you may hear the sound of thunder cracking, or if you receive your symbols through your clairsentience, you might intuitively feel wind blowing and rain falling. This, then, can be your symbol for a business partnership that will not be easy. The storm is pretty generic and may be a rather common symbol for this. However, it's also possible you will have a different symbol for a tumultuous business relationship. Maybe it would be an image of a broken contract or even a bank statement showing a huge drop in the cash balance. Invoked by something in your life, a memory or a thought, it will be something that somehow represents this type of business outcome for you.

### *Try This!*
### Your Symbols Journal

You need somewhere besides your mind to consolidate your symbols. You should go a step further if you want to be able to successfully translate your symbolic messages. Let's take a look at what will be your symbols. In the chart below, there are messages you may possibly get as you tune in to your intuition. Next to them, or in your own journal, record what immediately comes to mind as the symbolic representation for that particular message.

| Message | Symbols |
| --- | --- |
| Bad move | |
| Create a new product | |
| Failure | |
| Happiness | |
| Healthy | |
| Hire a particular employee | |
| Male or female | |
| Negative finances | |
| Nighttime | |
| Phone call | |

| Message | Symbols |
|---|---|
| Positive finances | |
| Positive relationship | |
| Quit your job | |
| Sell your property | |
| Start a business | |
| Stay | |
| Success | |
| Take a new job | |
| Take on a new client | |
| Wait | |

It is always a great idea to create your own journal, and it's a simple way to go deeper into your intuition. Write down any other symbols you interpret for your business or personal life along with any symbolic images from dreams. Using a computer, you can easily alphabetize your journal each time you update it with a new impression. In my book *The Book of Psychic Symbols*, I share a symbolic dictionary with over 500 meanings that might help you decipher a lot of what is happening in your dreams as well as your conscious intuitive symbols.

Creating your own journal will help you understand the impressions you pick up on. Getting a jump-start on your symbols journal will make it easier for you as you go forward. One of the best ways to do this is to merge your impressions with the information you get when you do external research, as in looking in a dictionary of symbols and adding to it your own translations. It must work for you—my interpretations or anyone else's should not negate what you pick up from your own observations. With each impression, your intuitive awareness will grow and can help to clarify answers you need in your business and personal life.

This journal can end up being one of your most valuable intuitive tools. Intuitive development will expand exponentially when you take advantage of the various tools that are available to you. As proficient as you become using your clair senses, there's always room to expand your intuitive knowledge.

## More Tools

You have options. You can choose from a variety of tools to increase your ability to tune in to your intuitive senses. Though some may call it cheating, it is really an opportunity to enhance and validate your gifts, another way to open your psychic receptors. When you are looking for more clarity, sometimes it is beneficial to make use of a combination of methods to enhance your perception. Let's look at what is out there.

### Oracle Cards

There are so many oracle cards available nowadays. From tarot cards to my own Psychic Symbols Oracle Cards, you'll find just about any type of oracle card you want. Oracle cards, essentially, are used to divine messages. They are usually a combination of colors and images and even words. It can take many years to learn how to do in-depth readings with them; however, you can use your basic knowledge and interpret what you see on the card and how they make you feel.

Using oracle cards as a tool can activate your intuition. They won't make you psychic, but they make it easier to access your abilities. If you need answers quickly, pulling a card or two can provide you with the basic information you may need. They provide you with an intuitive channel to get you rolling.

For example, let's pretend you are using my deck of cards. On each one, there are brightly colored images along with a simple description of what the card means. You have a decision to make—you need to decide whether to stay where you are at work or try to get a better job. The thing is, you're not sure how you'd be able to get a better job because you don't have the qualifications you need to move up. But your intuition is telling you that it may be time to do something different.

You pull a card to gain more insight. Interestingly, the one you pull is the School card. This gives you an immediate answer to both of your main questions. It is time for you to try to get a better job. However, it is an indication that you need to also get some additional training or go back to school in order to get that job. With one card, you've addressed both issues. Not pulling the card would have left you questioning what you should do or doubting your intuitive vibes. By utilizing your tool, you've not only validated your feelings on pursuing a better job, you've also gotten direction on how to do it.

Often, when I teach workshops or do book events I will offer the opportunity to my students to ask a question or two. Generally, if I want to be able to get to a lot of people I will pull a card or two to gain knowledge about them quickly. Looking at the card and the general meaning gives me a jumping-off point to immediately get right to the heart of the matter. For instance, I could have two different people ask two different questions, as happened during one of my signings.

As I was wrapping up the book event, the audience was asking questions. Because there were about seventy people there, I knew I had to intuit answers quickly, as we were already running over on time. I pulled out my card deck and called on the first person with their hand up.

"I would love to know if I am wasting my time with my boyfriend. I am really in love, but I'm not sure if he wants to settle down with me or not. I need to know!" Hannah exclaimed, with a sort of nervous giggle.

"Hmmm, let's see!" I told her.

I shuffled the cards in my hands until it felt like I should stop. Then I pulled the card.

"Well, look at this! I think this is a definite answer! I don't even need to translate it!" I laughed.

I had pulled the Diamond card. It was pretty obvious that my psychic symbols cards were telling Hannah there would be a diamond ring on the way. For this, I didn't have to decipher what else the card meant. In fact, the only thing I had to do was ask my guides to help me connect to the universal energy so I could pull the correct card for her. My guides had shown up and conspired to let her know to hang in there. The relationship was absolutely worth it, and Hannah was very happy to hear it!

I moved on to the next person.

"I would like to know about my start-up business. I don't know if it's going to work. I'm putting everything I have into it and barely sleeping, but everyone's telling me it's not worth it. I'm so stressed—I think they may be right," Sam said.

"Okay, good question. I am going to start shuffling. You tell me when to stop," I instructed her.

I wanted my energy to mix with hers in order to pull the best possible card to answer her question.

"Stop!" Sam said, a bit frenzied. "I'm nervous! Are you sure you don't want to choose for me?"

"We are connecting to our guides together. This will give us the best probable outcome," I told her.

I chuckled a bit when I flipped the card over. The audience had a puzzled look on their faces. And poor Sam. She didn't understand or know what to make of it. I explained.

"The diamond is not just about getting married. Diamonds are formed from coal. They are squeezed and put under a tremendous amount of constant pressure. They are put through intense stress in order to create something so beautiful and incredible. The value is exposed after the difficulty is endured, much like the value of your business. You are going through a lot of pressure right now, but it will be worth it in the end. Your business will be profitable if you put in a lot of effort right now," I told Sam.

Sam was excited, and everyone was surprised. The same card was picked for both Sam and Hannah. However, the symbolic meaning was different for each. This shows you that your symbols, cards or otherwise, can have multiple meanings.

### Try This!
### Pick an Oracle Card

While not everyone will own a deck of cards, there are multiple websites you can use to pull a card. If you go to my home page (Melanie Barnum.com), you will see an opportunity to click on a card for your

day. You can also visit www.colettebaronreid.com/use-colettes-free
-online-oracle-cards-app to utilize a couple of great card options from
Colette Baron Reid, a world-renowned psychic, medium, author, and
intuitive. Use this or your own oracle card deck for this exercise. Regardless of which method you use, be ready to pick your card.

Think of a situation or a specific question you have about your
work or your business. Try to stay away from yes-or-no questions.
What you are trying to do is get feedback or direction about the question. You are looking for answers that will point you in the best possible direction. You can ask, what would happen if I changed jobs? What
would the outcome be if I applied for a promotion? What would it be
like if I hired a new employee? How would it effect my business if I
fire my employee? What positive changes would there be if I were to
do more on social media? How difficult would it be if I went back to
school? What should I write my book about? What should I focus on?

When you've decided on your question, repeat it over and over
again either out loud or in your mind as you shuffle the cards. When
you are ready for the answer, choose your card. Immediately begin
observing the following:

- What was your first reaction?
- What is the card name or title?
- What colors are on the card?
- What images do you see?
- What other words or descriptions are there?
- How does the card make you feel?
- Do you hear anything while you're looking at it?
  Or if you hold it while closing your eyes?
- Does the card feel warm or cold or are there any
  vibrations coming off the card?
- Overall, what do you intuit from the
  card with regard to your question?

Now, apply your question to what you are picking up from the card. For example, let's pretend my question was "How can I expand my business?" and I picked the Books card. Now, using my intuition, I'll examine the questions one by one, adjusting the questions a bit to address the relation to my question and my card.

**What was your first reaction?**

"Of course I get the Books card! I am literally in the middle of writing another book and already have ideas for another."

**What is the card name or title, and what does it mean to you?**

"Books—it means to read and write books. Knowledge, gaining wisdom, and sharing wisdom."

**What colors are on the card, and what do they mean to you?**

"The main colors are blue, red, and black. Blue represents communication, speaking, and emotion. Red is about my foundation, or structure. It can also represent stress or frustration, especially along with the black."

**What do the images mean to you?**

"It shows me that multiple books are a good idea. It also tells me I need to continue learning more. I also see pale, rainbow-like colors in the distance, which tells me there are good things coming if I listen to my intuition. There are bright white fireworks and stars, which let me know my guides and loved ones are there to help me be successful."

**What other words or descriptions are there, and what do they mean for you?**

"They are telling me to increase my knowledge and then to teach what I've learned, so this makes sense to me. I've been thinking about offering more workshops, but I wasn't sure what to do. Maybe I can teach some classes based on my books. Maybe, also, I can incorporate some of what I learn from doing some research to offer better, fuller classes. I also feel like I can offer them online."

### How does the card make you feel with regard to your question?

"I feel like I am kind of recharged or energized. It feels like this is possible, like I can actually accomplish this! I feel like I am being called to teach other people and I like that."

### Do you hear anything while you're looking at it? Or if you hold it while closing your eyes?

"I hear fireworks, like explosions of positive energy. I hear whispers coming from the books, kind of inviting me to open them."

### Does the card feel warm or cold or are there any vibrations coming off the card?

"I am not really feeling temperature, though it feels almost cool and fresh, and it kind of feels like there is a really high vibration—kind of a fast buzz."

### Now, overall, what do you intuit from pulling the card with regard to your question?

"I feel like I am headed in the right direction. It feels like I can continue to write and do some more research on what I want to expand upon as far as growth. I also feel like now is a great time for me to expand through teaching workshops and sharing my knowledge. I feel like it would be a successful endeavor, and I feel like that would expand my client base. Overall, I feel like it is a positive card for me!"

Based on my example, you can look at your own card and glean the answers for yourself. Obviously, if someone asked, "What should I do with my life?" and they were contemplating writing a book for the first time, pulling the Books card would be interpreted a bit differently. They would probably take it as a message to get started with their novel. Using your intuition along with the power of symbolism, you can gain a lot of direction from pulling just a single card, especially when it can be hard to trust your intuition without something tangible to validate it.

Remember, your helpers want to boost your intuitive awareness. They are totally on board with you using whatever tools you can in order to interpret their messages with more clarity. The more concisely you can decipher what you're intuiting, the greater chance you have of following your best possible path. By tuning in to your intuition, you are completing a connection to the universe. Doing this can provide you with incredible gains while providing you with something a bit more tangible to see or hold. And, speaking of more tangible, psychometry can be exactly what you need to get to your next intuitive level.

## Psychometry

No matter the method, you're discovering different approaches to tuning in to your intuition. While there are many, there is one more that we'll talk about. *Psychometry* is a tool used to connect us to a person, place, thing, or situation. Essentially, psychometry is based on the fact that objects hold energy (see chapter 5 for more on energy). By holding or touching an object, you can gain information intuitively about it or people connected to it. Often photographs are used to connect to someone or to intuit circumstances around them. Jewelry is also often used because metal tends to hold on to energy the best. However, you can get mostly everything you want to know by holding on to something having to do with what you are trying to understand.

This can come in handy in professional situations. If someone is coming to you with a product they are trying to sell to you, it would be a huge advantage if you could intuitively read the background of that person or the item they are offering. Think of this as a catalyst to connect you quickly without having to create a connection.

Here's an example: Michael was a bartender. He was offered two jobs within a week of each other. They were both new bars and he didn't know anything about them. The first bar, the Outpost, had felt good when he went in. He liked the way the place was laid out, and it seemed like the owners were pretty cool. He was getting kind of excited about it. Then he went to the second bar, the Trapdoor. Again, he felt comfortable and enjoyed the interview, and the layout was great there too. He was offered essentially the same deal at both places making it that much more difficult to choose.

Michael decided to use psychometry. He took napkins from both locations when he went in for his interviews. Each napkin had the bar's name on it. He tuned in and asked his intuition to connect.

He knew from his visits, and the napkins confirmed, that the owners from both places were good people. He also picked up on a busy energy for both places. That was good: that meant a lot of tips and he would get a lot of hours. He still couldn't decide, so he took turns with each napkin, just holding it and sitting in silence. The napkin for the Outpost felt fine. He felt like it just validated what he already felt. He moved on to the Trapdoor. At first, it pretty much felt the same. Then, all of a sudden, he saw a whoosh of water and heard a breaking sound. He didn't know what it meant, but it didn't feel good.

Michael chose to go with the Outpost. A month after he started his job there, he felt like it was a second home. He enjoyed the work and liked the people even more. It seemed he had made the right decision. His intuition was confirmed when he turned on the news and saw that the Trapdoor's roof had collapsed and the whole building caught on fire. They were out of business and probably wouldn't reopen. Though Michael felt bad for them, he was happy he had intuited what he had from using psychometry.

## Will We Always Be Right?

Thankfully, Michael was right. He was able to interpret his intuitive messages correctly. This is not always the case, though. We will not be 100 percent accurate, and this is normal. What happens if we're wrong? That depends on the situation. If you find yourself unsure of your intuition, back it up with other data. Cut yourself some slack. You are working hard to tap in. Sometimes it'll feel like you've got it but you're actually wrong, and other times it will feel like you just can't seem to figure it out. Either way, that's okay. The universe is trying to help you, so trust that as you develop, you will get more accurate, as long as you believe in the possibility.

We are trying to interpret information across a different dimension or plane of existence. Occasionally, obviously, we will get it wrong. We can even go so far as to admit we may just miss what our intuition is telling us altogether. The most important thing about getting it wrong is not giving up. Stay open to the vibes you are receiving. Remember, your intuitive gifts are there for you, no one else. It may not be as natural for you to interpret your vibes correctly, so using your tools may come in handy!

As you've read, learning to decipher symbols is a critical part of helping you to become intuitively aware. Tools such as oracle cards are easier to interpret using the symbolic language our messengers send us. Symbolism can be simple and self-explanatory, or it can be complex and derived from extremely personal references. This is why it is so beneficial for you to create your symbols journal. You can refer to it to help you translate the messages you intuit for yourself in business or your personal life.

You have the power—only you—to access your gifts. No one can take that away from you. Knowing that you can use your developing abilities in business allows you to believe that you can, for sure, be fierce. You have nothing to apologize for; in fact, it's just the opposite. Tapping into your intuition to help you get ahead is smart, though sometimes we are so busy we don't slow down enough to recognize the messages that are coming through, which is why, frequently, you'll find your messengers are working overtime to get messages to you, even when you're sleeping.

# Chapter 3
# Pulling Your Intuitive Awareness from Dreams

*Our dreams can be deeply powerful intuitive messengers that hold keys*
*and clues to our deepest selves. Far beyond their ability to amuse or terrify us,*
*they hold a profound communication system that when we learn to*
*understand we can use to heal and transform our lives.*

—SIMONE WRIGHT

Another common way people experience intuition is through dreams. We all dream. Whether we remember our dreams or not is a different story. When you wake up and feel like the dream you had was real life, that is usually more than a regular dream. That is your spirit's way of letting you know something, and often that something is about what is to come. Premonitory dreams, or precognitive dreams, happen to alert you or let you know what may be developing in the future. Sometimes they are symbolic and must be deciphered entirely. Other dreams may lay things out in more detail. It may be a mix of both.

Our dreams come from a myriad of sources. They are a way for our subconscious to process problems or dilemmas or even details of the day that we haven't figured out while awake. Dreaming is also a way for our deceased loved ones and spirit guides to visit—and for our intuition to come through.

Sometimes life is so hectic we don't notice our intuitive vibes trying to come through, or we ignore what we are picking up. Our subconscious, sleepy mind can help us get out of our own way to allow our intuitive awareness to open up through our dreams.

## Processing Life

We are so busy. We are always doing. Maybe it's working or taking care of our kids, or maybe it's going out and playing. Maybe it's staying home and trying to figure out how to pay the bills. We even focus so much energy on our diet—how to gain and how to lose weight and eat healthy doing it. Sometimes—let's be honest—we can't even remember what the heck it is that we spend our time doing but we know we are busy. We don't always have time to figure things out—actually, it's more that we don't allocate time toward tuning in to what may be significant in our lives. That's where intuitive dreams can come in, to process our lives.

Patty, a friend as well as a client, came in for a reading. I was doing her reading, explaining all the details I was picking up. All was going well, but then I stopped.

"What's with the dreams?" I asked her.

"What do you mean?" she responded.

"I feel like you are receiving messages in your dreams. I think you need to pay attention to them. It's like you are processing things while you sleep because your conscious mind doesn't have the energy to explore it."

"I have no idea what you're talking about." Patty chuckled. I wasn't sure if she was being serious because she had a comedic manner, and that fun attitude carried through here.

"Okay, well, let's see."

I tuned in to her energy. Suddenly, I got the feeling that there was something really wrong with her body chemistry. I could sense that overall something was happening inside her, and it was not as it was supposed to happen. I wasn't quite sure yet what it was. Then it hit me.

"Have you been dreaming of taking medicine?"

"That's bizarre! I had this dream where I was about to take my meds, and I kept dropping them on the ground," she said, this time with a more serious face.

"Your intuition is telling you something," I told her.

"Huh? What do you mean?"

I went on to explain that I felt she was taking something that wasn't right. At first, I suggested it might be that she needed to adjust her dose. Then it came in more clearly, so I told her she needed to see her doctor right away because something didn't feel right with her medication. I asked her if she had recently started this new medicine, and she stated she'd been on it for a couple of months and that she didn't feel quite right since taking it.

Patty said she would check it out. She put the medicine issue on the back burner for a bit. She texted me a couple months later to let me know what was happening. Knowing I rarely remember readings, she spelled it out for me: "You (and my spirit guides) told me I was taking the wrong meds or the wrong prescription. Last week I found out my doctor had prescribed the meds and the dosage incorrectly! What the heck?! When I asked the doctor about what I was taking, he looked like he saw a ghost. We spoke in his office about how he had originally told me to take the medication versus how the medication should actually have been taken, and it was then I realized you were 100 percent correct. He told me to stop taking it immediately. I don't need it. The doctor confirmed it is not for me! Thank you so much!"

Patty's text to me was great. I was so glad I was able to tune in to see what was happening with her body chemistry, which helped me understand what was happening. However, that was not the only thing to pay attention to here, and I told Patty as much.

"You are so welcome. But take a second to think back. Do you remember talking about your dreams? You said in your dream you kept trying to take your medicine, but it was falling on the floor. That was your intuition trying to get your attention to notice something was not quite right with your prescription," I shared. "You knew it intuitively—you just hadn't recognized it, yet!"

Patty's intuitive guidance system was trying to let her know something was wrong and used her subconscious to try and share it with her. "Intuition is our means of tuning in to truths about our health that the conscious mind cannot know or is denying," writes Char Margolis, psychic, author, and television personality.[7] Patty's dream state was the only place she slowed down long enough to receive the message, as she was so busy every day. I am convinced that had she not come in when she did, she would have put two and two together and figured out what her intuition was telling her. It just would have taken a bit longer.

Your dreams can help you process life in so many different ways. From how to handle medicine, like in Patty's case, to dealing with your finances, and everything in between, your intuition will often play out the story of what you're dealing with in your dreams. It may be the only time you slow down enough to receive the intuitive messages.

## Premonitions and Dreams

Betsy has the premonitory type of dreams. She's had them sporadically throughout the years—probably more than she realizes. We were discussing intuition during a Goddess Weekend, during which about twenty of us strong, beautiful women got together to bond over our incredibly powerful energy. We started sharing stories.

Betsy said, "I have one, but I don't know if this is my intuition or not."

Well, of course I wanted to know all about it. She shared her first story with us. Shortly before Thanksgiving, Betsy had a dream. In the dream she realized she was being told to be sure her CPR training was up to date and that she remembered how to do it. She had no idea what that meant, but she woke up with the desire to be sure she knew how to perform CPR in order to help anyone in need. She didn't have to wait long to try it out.

Betsy's workplace had an annual Thanksgiving meal. During the gathering, the owner of the business started to choke. Betsy's coworker quickly performed the Heimlich maneuver, but he did it wrong. Rather than helping dislodge what she was choking on, he actually pushed the air out of her lungs. Betsy's training kicked in. She knew, as scary as it was, that she needed

---

7. Char Margolis, *Discover Your Inner Wisdom: Using Intuition, Logic, and Common Sense to Make Your Best Choices* (New York: Fireside, 2008), 67.

to let her boss and mentor pass out. She had learned it would relax her muscles in her neck and throat. Sure enough, her boss passed out and Betsy was able to reach in and remove what was blocking her airway.

Her premonitory dream had prepared her for what was to come. It had caused her to brush up on her knowledge, which pretty much led to her saving her mentor's life. Not only had her intuition come through in a dream, but it came through with a precognitive and precautionary warning. Thankfully, she had listened to her dream.

## Paying Attention to
## Recurring Dreams with Warnings

We've got so much going on in our lives that we often neglect our intuition. Sometimes it seems like it takes too much effort to merely notice our intuitive hits. When we don't recognize important messages while awake, our intuitive guidance is going to find a way to come through, so showing up in our dreams makes a lot of sense. There are other types of intuitive dreams besides ones that are precognitive. There are also nightmares. These are dreams that may happen as a wake-up call or to help you process real-life trauma. Nightmares can also reflect crisis or fear. This type of intuitive message can also bring warnings of current health issues.

Meghan, a forty-two-year-old mother of three teenage boys, had a real wake-up call. Her intuition came through in her dreams in the form of recurring nightmares. Out of the blue, one night she had a dream that she was pulled into rapids and was repeatedly being smashed up against huge rocks. The dream was so real and so forceful it woke her up, gasping for breath and holding her left side in pain. The pain in her side continued for hours—so severely at times that it caused her to break down in tears. Then, just like that, it went away.

About a week later, Meghan had the same dream and woke up again in unbearable pain. As before, the pain lasted for a few hours. It was intense. She began feeling like something may be wrong. She wanted to see her doctor but had just recently been in for a full physical, gynecological exam, and blood work. They hadn't found anything wrong, and her husband felt she was overreacting.

Flash forward to about two weeks later. Meghan had the dream again—but this time she wasn't just smashed against rocks, she was also pulled under by seaweed. Like before, she woke up out of breath. She was in such intense pain she decided to call the doctor that day. The best they could do was more blood work and an ultrasound, since she had just had a full physical only a few weeks prior with no red flags.

A few days went by and she received a phone call from the nurse's office telling her that her blood work and ultrasound had come back fine. That night, she had the dream again, only this time there was a blur or shadow-type figure standing at the side of the rapid waters. It was screaming something she couldn't fully hear but sounded like "tubes." When she woke, she had the same intense pain. What the hell was happening? She was becoming afraid to sleep!

She called her doctor and spoke to him about the intense pain and asked if there was another type of ultrasound that would look specifically at her fallopian tubes. He told her to come in for an endovaginal ultrasound. As she watched the screen, the nurse gasped. It turned out there was a cancerous cyst in her fallopian tube the size of a grapefruit. She went in to have it removed immediately. The doctor told her if she hadn't had it removed, or if it had gone undiagnosed even a few more weeks, her chances of survival would have been bleak.

I have no idea why the cancer didn't show up in the bloodwork, but I do know that Meghan's intuitive nightmares had let her know something was indeed wrong. If they hadn't continued alerting her and drumming up the pain, she might never have found the cancer. Meghan persisted and she's still here to share her story of intuition. Not only did she use it, but she is now a survivor.

## Dream Symbolism

Interpreting dreams can be tricky. They can be literal translations of what's happening in your life, showing up to help you process what's happening while awake, or they can quite often be symbolic. In Meghan's experience, water was a symbol in each dream. Water typically represents emotions. However, it can represent your plumbing—in your house or in your body. The rapids indicated there was something tumultuous and probably painful going on, and boy, was there!

The symbols that show up in dreams are not always as easy to recognize for what they represent. For example, the water in Meghan's dream is easily decipherable as her plumbing after the fact. During the dream, it can be more difficult to understand. Referencing a dream dictionary or your symbols book is a great way to start understanding your future night messages. An entry in Meghan's journal would look something like this:

*Water:* Can represent emotions, building plumbing, or anatomical plumbing

*Water, Rapids:* Can represent turmoil or an issue with the above, something that is causing grief and must be addressed

## Figuring Out Relationships, Personal and Professional

Mary had recurring nightmares. She had dreams that she wasn't quite sure were her intuition speaking to her or her subconscious mind sending her a message, but she knew it was something to listen to. For weeks, night after night, she dreamt about spiders dropping from the ceiling on top of her while in bed. The sensation was so real every single night. She continually jumped out of bed, often climbing over her husband who was sleeping beside her.

The dream was so real and never varied, repeatedly. The spiders would drop from the ceiling, landing on her. She knew there was something deeper going on and was pretty sure it was a sign to take some action.

She had been contemplating quitting her long-term job, which had become more of a familial type relationship than a company position. Her friends had previously talked her out of it three years before, citing how long she'd been there and how it was like working with family. But no matter what she did, nothing got better in her increasingly bad work environment. The stress and anxiety of having to deal with a boss who was an out-in-the-open liar, a drinker, and a drug user just wore her down. She knew subconsciously this dream was her mind shouting at her to get out. Be it a web of lies or a spiderweb, she knew it was time to leave. The repetitive spiders finally convinced her. She sat down with her boss and told him she was done. She never looked back. She experienced peace of mind and started living the life she wanted with no regrets, thankful that the spiders had showed up for her.

Mary was lucky. She recognized the spiders as a portent of things to come and what she was dealing with. Her emotions were playing out in her intuitive dreams and she knew she had to act. It was hard enough dealing with her own problems in her personal life, but not dealing with the work issues had caused her sleepless nights and scary imagery. As soon as Mary made her decision after that last nightmare, the spiders disappeared, and she was able to get a full night's sleep again.

Think of dreams as your gateway into intuition. When we don't get it during consciousness, we are afforded an opportunity to review what our sixth sense is trying to tell us while we are asleep. We aren't always as astute with our ESP as we'd like to be, but don't worry—our intuitive vibes will keep coming!

We are connected to the energy of the universe, and our guides will give us the information we need, regardless of whether we are awake or asleep. We are beginning an incredible period of growth. There is no perfect method to decide who we want to bring along during this time, but reading the energy of others allows us to examine who works best in our lives.

# CHAPTER 4
# Feeling the Energetic Handshake

*When you learn the native language of your own distinct energy field,*
*you become able to read it, hear it and converse with it.*
*One of the trickiest things in cultivating new sensibilities*
*about your own and other people's energies is that they often*
*don't show up in the ways you expect them.*

—DONNA EDEN AND DAVID FEINSTEIN, *ENERGY MEDICINE*

Handshakes are one of the most common forms of greeting another person. More often than not, it is the way we are introduced or introduce ourselves to others, and is our first line of communication with someone new. It is also a great way to acquaint ourselves with the other person's energy. When we touch someone, it's like we have an express connection to their metaphysical power, their own energy, and we have the ability to discover what motivates them. We can tap into their spirit and essentially get a quick snapshot of who they are, the kind of person they are, and even whether we can trust them. It is a powerful and rapid way to allow our intuition to guide us, and, yes, tell us whether we like the person or not.

This chapter shares the nine basic types of people you'll be shaking hands with. Of course, there are always outliers or those who defy categorization.

Those are usually a combination of types. Gathering data from the people you shake hands with is an invaluable tool in life and, more specifically, business. Deciphering their energy, upon first introduction, gives your intuitive support system the opportunity to facilitate the meeting. By learning to read the energy, you are accelerating your knowledge of the type of person you are dealing with, which gives you an upper hand. There is so much you can learn from this common greeting that from now on you should be sure to shake the hand of everyone you meet—that is, if you're smart and want to gain as much insight as you can.

Interestingly enough, you can gain information from a hug or even a fist bump, but it won't be the same. The reason is because with a handshake, the two people are generally saying, "Hey, I'm here. This is me," and they are extending their energy intentionally. With a hug, it's more of a comforting thing, and it changes the energy you are receiving. You can gather knowledge from any type of touch, but to really pick up what they are putting out, the handshake will be the best form. And, most often you won't be hugging in business, but you will be shaking hands.

Your gut instinct, or your clairsentience, is the first line of communication with the handshaker's energy. You can pick up on their vibe by checking in with how your body feels and how they make you feel. Just like when you worked with your clairs in chapter 2, you can use those same methods to perceive the energy of the people you are dealing with. Again, you'll gain an advantage by understanding who you are dealing with before you put a lot of effort into the professional or personal relationship.

## The Handshakers

Basically, there are nine types of people in this world when it comes to the handshake. You've probably met at least a couple of these people on your journey through life and possibly even experienced combinations of them. They may conjure up images in your mind of real people, or they may make you see a stereotypical version in your imagination when you read about them below—this is wonderful! Allow that to happen, as this is your mind's eye, your intuitive senses, explaining who they are to you.

### The Eager Beaver

This is the one who is so eager to please, so excited to be able to do whatever you want or need, that they can't contain themselves. You can feel their energy pulsing through your hand as they pump your arm up and down. They continue in this vein until you actually make them stop. This person easily and simply exposes themselves to you—they are there to help you and will be enthusiastic the whole time. Unfortunately, for some, this can get annoying very quickly if it continues. However, it can be an ego boost, at least temporarily, when someone essentially worships you and is so incredibly grateful that you are giving them the opportunity to be in your presence and do something they really want to do. The feeling of their energy reminds me of a happy puppy! Can you see that? Or feel it?

### The Confident One

This person wants you to know they've got it together, but not in a bad way. It's like they exude their confidence through that handshake. You can feel how comfortable they are. They pretty much know who they are, and they're okay with it, at least in this particular situation. Their self-assured energy comes through and makes you feel comfortable. These people want to succeed and know that they can. Imagine shaking that person's hand and seeing them—the way they casually wear their clothes perfectly, not a hair out of place—smiling at you, knowing everything will turn out well. They are well aware of how others should and do respect them for all their current and future accomplishments. You can feel how put together they are, especially if you're not!

### The Smarmy One

We have all dealt with this one. You know who I'm talking about, the one with the wimpy handshake. I'm not talking about someone who is trying to be respectful and not squeeze too hard—no. I mean the wet noodle handshake, the person who's throwing off a creepy vibe. This is the person who makes you uncomfortable in the worst way, who you can feel is instantly looking you up and down, sizing you up. This person makes you feel like they are putting their napkin in their collar, getting ready to feast on your energy. You almost instantly distrust them, even if you've never met them or heard of them. You can just feel their smarminess oozing out of their pores, and you just don't like them.

### The Respectful One

This is the person who is deferential, the one who lets you know, with their handshake, that they respect who you are. They know you are worthy of admiration and are almost reverent in the way they look at you. They are not, however, disingenuous. They are real and courteous. They might even go beyond being polite and can come across as almost submissive. These are the people who are ready to help and will do what you need, because they value your intelligence and your standing. You know who I'm talking about. This person, you just know, will stand by you because they have been taught that there is a hierarchy and they accept that. Not that they will give up their own personality or life for yours, but they believe they need to follow your directive without talking behind your back.

### The Oh So Cocky Person

Oh, this one. This person is annoying as hell. This is one you can clearly feel thinks they know it all. They totally believe they know better than anyone else, and they are going to prove it to you, even if they can't. They want to show you just how great they are. This individual wants you to know that they can do anything and they are the best one for the job. They will interrupt anyone to prove a point and they will fight about being right by being loud and even obnoxious. You all know this person. Heck, you may even be this person. But this goes beyond confidence: this is pure ego, and you can feel it in their handshake when they try to make you feel less than or smaller than them in every way. You might even feel belittled, merely by the energy they send through to you. They have total indifference for the wisdom you may have, regardless of whether they believe you know what you are doing or not. This person believes they are all that, even when they aren't.

### The Unasked for Sexual One

This person is the reason for the Me Too movement. They are sexual and might even rub you with their fingers in an overtly sexual way. They make you feel like a piece of meat simply by the way they hold your hand and leer at you. They are pervasive instantly and leave you feeling dirty even from just a brief handshake. On a lighter note, this person may try to win you over by being flirty, but all that does is make you uncomfortable. They have a blatant disregard for boundaries and consider their suggestive tone to be flattering to you. This person considers besting you in business to be similar to a sexual conquest and wants to win. They think they are doing you a favor by slyly seducing you with their charms.

### The Caring One

This person's handshake exudes kindness. It is a compassionate feeling that extends all the way through your arm up to your heart. They are a sensitive person and an empathetic person who you instantly feel comfortable with. They want to help you. They want you to be okay and are concerned with making you feel appreciated. They want to help you reach your goals in an interested way and will nurture your ideas as their own. They will tend to your needs and your wishes because they want you to succeed. They like everything to be nice for you and you can feel their positive energy as they send it through their handshake. The only problem with them is their caring can feel suffocating if it's not balanced. After all, there's a time and place for nurturing.

### The Friendly One

So friendly. Warm and inviting. You find yourself instantly wanting to share your entire life story with them. They are welcoming and make you feel comfortable right off the bat. They make you feel like they will help you with whatever you need. They will assist you in any way they can in order to make your life easier. It's almost like shaking the hand of someone you already know. It feels like you suddenly have a telepathic connection to them. This is someone you want on your side; they will work hard for you and will connect well with your clients. They make people feel relaxed and happy, and you for sure need that.

### The Nervous One

Their energy is infectious, but not in a good way. You feel a buzz coming from their hand, and it evokes feelings of being trapped. This is not necessarily someone you want shaking the hands of your customers because they transmit panic. They might very well be fine after they get to know you, but it's as though they are hiding something and are afraid you'll know what it is from the mere touch of your hands. They might be moist (yes, I said that) to the touch, and you can imagine seeing the glistening sweat dripping from their brow. Just thinking of this person makes you feel a bit jumpy and unsure of yourself and what they, and you, can bring to the table. This is not someone who brings to mind the confidence you need.

## Intuitive Insight for Whether or Not to Trust

What do you do with all the stuff you discovered when you shook hands? How does all that energy—which, by the way, can be a little overwhelming if you don't protect yourself (see chapter 1)—affect you and how you do business? Well, first, you learn if you can trust them.

Trust can be a scary thing in the business world. There are many who will attempt to manipulate you in order to control the situation. These two simple words, *Trust me*, denote a question in your mind as to whether the person who said them is being truthful. Think about when you've heard someone ask you to trust them. Immediately, it brings up a strong desire to know what the heck is going on. Honesty is a very expensive gift, and there are many people who aren't interested in giving you all that much when they are trying to get ahead. Being able to read the energy of the person you're with makes it much easier to discern whether they are full of it or being genuine.

Think back to the handshakes. Out of the nine types, which ones would you think you'd automatically trust or not trust? The more you're able to read from the initial meeting of energy with the other person, the easier it is to discover how trustworthy they actually are and whether you want them in your corner or not. Worst-case scenario, you have to discern if they would stab you in the back or have your back. Interpreting what type of person they are, at least primarily, impresses upon you whether you can rely on them and believe in them.

## Intuitive Insight for Realizing Worth

Beyond trusting that someone is being honest with you, how do you determine they are actually worthy of your energy? Is the business deal worthy of your time? Is the project you're being pitched worthy of your consideration? When you rely totally on the regular process, you are counting on research and analytics to make your decisions. When you instead allow yourself to tune in to your intuition, you acknowledge that this nontraditional process will grant you access to a different method you can use to ascertain whether this is, indeed, worthy of your energy at all or would be a waste. It's time for you to step out on the limb and listen to your what your vibes are telling you!

On the other end of the spectrum, do you know your worth? You damn well better! Knowing your worth is just as important, if not more important, than judging another's worthiness. You need to believe in your value, in what you have to offer to someone else. Working with others is not merely transactional in one specific instance—it is long term. When you realize your worth, your energy shifts, which in turn attracts new people, and what do you know?! You've declared, through your energy, that you deserve more.

The handshake connects you to the other person physically and energetically. As you've discovered already, it can tell you what type of person they are in mere seconds. It can also help you decipher their traits as they relate to what you need from them. So take it further by examining some simple questions.

### Try This!
### Gaining More Insight from the Greeting

Using this method to go deeper into your intuition becomes easier the more you do it, and it can be used to discover whether to trust the person as well as determining their worthiness. Though you only have a moment initially to take in the essence of someone you are meeting, you can continue tuning in to their energy by immediately asking any relevant questions in your mind. In addition, when you ask the questions, you are stimulating your intuition, which can make opening your awareness to the impressions you receive simpler. Take a look at these questions and use them as an easy guide to start tapping into your responses metaphysically now and in the future.

- What do you feel about the energy of the other person?
- Can you tell what type of person you are shaking hands with?
- What images do you see in your mind's eye?
- What sounds, names, songs, and so on do you hear?
- What do you know about the person?
- Can you trust them?
- Are they good for you?
- Do they have your back?
- Does it feel natural for you to want to tell them about yourself?
- Do you like them?
- Are they worthy of your friendship?
- Do they deserve to be hired?
- Is the person a hard worker?
- Do they have what you want?
- Can they accomplish what you need them to do?
- Are they worthy of your time?

This is not a complete list, but you get the basic gist. What we are doing here is learning to discern what you can pick up from the person you are meeting. There's no secret to how this works. However, the key really is learning how to get the best data the quickest. The questions you focus on can be more specific to why you are meeting the new person. For example, if you are being introduced to someone who is pitching a new product to you, you might want to focus on seeing the product (or something representing the product) on the shelf in your mind's eye. Does it look bright and exciting and shiny? Or does it look like it's gathered so much dust you'd suffer an asthma attack if you got anywhere near it? These two images can give you a pretty clear picture whether the proposed product is a good one or not.

Essentially, ask the questions that fit the situation, and then pay attention. What vibes are you picking up about the person or people you are meeting? Start with the simplest of simple: Do you like their energy? Take it from there. If you receive answers that turn you off, go deeper. Ask the universe why they give off that vibe. It may surprise you with a response you don't expect, which can also sway your opinion on what you are getting. You'll find you'll become more proficient with each handshake.

## Reading Energy for Desire and Motivation

Reading someone's energy can help you understand what drives them. We can tell pretty quickly if they are profit-centered or if there is more to it. Is it about just making a quick buck to put in their own pocket? Because screw that. You want to be successful and want it to last. If you could feel what they want and why and you know it's not just that they are trying to make enough money to pay their rent that month, that will change how you feel about the situation. Do your desires match up with theirs? Does what they want for their company coincide with what you want for yours?

This is a great time to leverage your intuition. Use it to discern what is driving the person you are dealing with. Let your intuition help you figure out what makes them tick. Like reading the energetic handshake, this is a perfect opportunity to take your vibes to the next level. Be thankful you are able to tune in to them by using your rapidly developing instincts. Asking the questions internally and waiting for an answer using your senses can be your first clue to what motivates them and if their needs are in alignment with yours.

### *Try This!*
### Learning How to Discern Yes or No

Let's practice by discerning simple answers. Start by feeling if you are drawn in one direction or the other for the following questions.

Using a yes/no scale can help you tune in to your clairsentience. For instance, see a horizontal line in your mind's eye with the word *yes* to the left of the line and the word *no* to the right. How do you know if they cross the center of the line and move toward either the yes or no? Ask a question such as "Are they motivated by money alone?" and then feel where your energy is drawn to on the line. You can also see with your clairvoyance where you are on the line. Chances are you won't be leaning all the way in either direction, but you may feel a slight tug going one way or the other. Once you are able to finalize where your answer is to the initial question, you can keep at it and find out other things about the person or people.

You can also use your ESP to ascertain their driving force for other reasons. Let's say your boss is telling you to do something, but you're not quite sure what they are looking for. When you tap into their energy, you can feel what motivates them and why they are asking for you to do what they need you to do. Are they asking you for something because they genuinely need it? If you are afraid they are deliberately trying to hold you back from success or are being vindictive or jealous in some way, wouldn't it be great if you were able to intuit the truth behind their motivation?

Knowing what they want from you and why can help you accomplish your task in a more complete and fulfilling way. Not only that, but how cool would it be to recognize where they are coming from? That would definitely score you some brownie points and help propel your career by showing them how incredibly shrewd you can be.

## It's Not Always about Business

Whether it's a business deal or a personal relationship, sometimes you must be ready to say to hell with it—be detached from the outcome. Be willing to understand that the job you are hoping for or the deal you are trying to close may not be the best thing for you. It might be that you don't get it because it would knock you off your path or because there is something better on its way. Be open to the idea that there may be something superior coming.

When you are fighting so hard for something because you deem, intellectually, that it is the best thing for you, it can wreak havoc with your intuition. You think it's what you need financially, and possibly to elevate your status in the business world, but while you're trying so hard to make it happen, you are drowning out your intuition telling you there may be something wrong with the deal you are trying to make or the contract you are trying to win or the job you are trying to get.

Getting out of your own way can allow for your metaphysical senses to bloom instead. Of course you're enthusiastic about the possibility of something great happening, but if you are so focused on what you think should happen, it makes it really difficult to go with the flow—and by flow I mean allowing your vibes to guide you without trouble. When you're so sure that something should have a positive outcome, it's challenging to be thankful for a negative result, but that's exactly what you need to be able to do.

Relationships are everywhere, and there are many types—business, partnership, professional, school, parental, sibling, and even love. We've pretty much all experienced breakups in some way, be they romantic or otherwise. I know I have! And most often those breakups are not easy to get over, especially the intimate type. They leave us with a really bad taste in our mouth and can make us feel like we screwed something up. It can also leave us feeling empty or alone and maybe, more often, can make us angry and pissed off. We either dumped them because they did something awful and they totally disrespected us, or they left us because, yup, they were just plain jerks. Either way, it can cause us a lot of grief. But all our relationships serve a purpose, and business partnerships can often feel as intimate as romantic ones.

I have a client who tried so hard, but she couldn't see past her current broken partnership to the possibility there may be something better. After the third connection imploded, she was grasping at straws, trying to hold on to her relationship because even though she knew each new partner had been better than the last, she believed this was it and there was no way she was going to get so lucky again. I told her to tune in to her intuition because I had already tuned in to mine and had seen the next connection would be the best connection. But I didn't tell her that. I wrote it down instead, along with the description of who it would be, and gave it to her to hold on to until she was ready to open it. Rather, I had her write a list of what she wanted in a new partnership.

So what did she do? She decided to try to listen to my advice. I mean, after all, she had come to me for a few readings and trusted everything I had told her so far. She was able to let go and move on without focusing on what was to come, believing now that directing her energy on herself was best. Within months, she met the partner of her dreams, the one she wanted to manifest. And when she opened the envelope I had given her, she realized it was the person I had tuned in to and that by trusting her own intuition, she had created the opportunity and space for a much better relationship. She stopped being fearful and let go of needing to know the outcome, and that, my friends, is an incredible intuitive victory.

There are so many ways to pick up on the energy of someone. As you can see, it can be done for a variety of reasons. It can all start with a simple hand-shake. From there, determining what's going on with the people you're deal-ing with is an easy transfer. Now, while I'm saying you can read their energy, I'm not saying that you'll always be right, meaning if you intuit something negative coming off them, you might have to look a bit deeper. It might just be that they are coming to you to try to make a great deal, but you are tuning in to the fact they are broke and desperate to make it work. So pay attention. If you feel something you don't like, ask the universe to give you some more information about the "why" before you walk away from something that could be mutually beneficial.

You are tapping into their energy—gaining what information you can from that connection. But you can also manipulate your own energy. You can choose to expand or even retract your energy based on the situation or what you are trying to accomplish. You might find you become even more moti-vated to succeed as you learn that employing practices such as meditation to help you control your energy and your aura can bring you to the next level of where you want to be.

# CHAPTER 5

# Expand Your Energy to Increase Your Overall Influence

*The first thing to realize is that you are in control of your own energy....*
*[Sources of energy] connect you to the flow of life,*
*which is constantly renewing itself.*

—DEEPAK CHOPRA

We talk about the biggest person in the room, the most influential person sitting at the table. There is no reason that person can't be you. You can expand your energy. This is ideal! How incredible would that be? Once you discover how to magnify your metaphysical aura, you can grow your overall influence to gain what you want or need to succeed in business.

I know it may sound like something that is beyond what you can do or even what you can easily bring yourself to believe in, but it is more than possible to change the way you can inspire others. When you increase your presence, you increase your impact. You want to be that person, the person with the influence, because that person is the one with the power, and that power can help you be the success you want to be. There are many ways you can expand your energy, but increasing your aura is one of the easiest methods.

But that's not all. You don't always want to limit yourself to just expanding your energy—you need to work on managing it. Meditation can provide you with the means you need to calm down. After all, you don't want to haphazardly overpower everyone in the room because you are out of control. It's not about total domination. Understanding how to expand but also steady your auric energy will keep you more balanced and composed no matter the situation or circumstance you find yourself in.

## What Is an Aura?

Every living thing has an aura. It is our energy field that emits from our physical body, usually about one to two inches outward around the body. This ethereal layer can be felt and even seen by others who are sensitive to energy, and it can be read intuitively, just like you did when you were doing the handshake mambo. It's kind of like our energetic skin. It can also magnify and grow or shrink in size depending on what we are doing or what we are thinking. This energetic stratum is what we feel in others when we say, "Wow, they have a huge presence!" We can manipulate auras once we learn how.

An aura will change constantly. It adjusts to our moods and our needs and desires. Think of your aura as kind of an energetic organ, which, while being part of your metaphysical body, is also strongly connected to your emotional and even physical self. Auras shift. They change. They can even be managed, somewhat. They can be used to expand your energetic footprint, thereby putting yourself out in the world as more powerful. With one adjustment, you can increase your confidence and feel more significant. And now you're wondering, "Great, but exactly how can you do it?" Well, hold on to your aura, because here we go!

Let's connect to your feelings in a different way. When you think of something that makes you really angry, and I mean really angry, what happens? Think back to a time when you were really pissed off. Maybe someone did you wrong in some way or someone messed with your kids or your family. Possibly your boss screwed you over or your coworker cheated you out of credit for something. How do you react? Does your breathing speed up? Slow down? Do you get warmer? If it's an argument with someone, do you lean toward them? Lean away? Talk through clenched teeth? Yell? Whisper? Ball your fists?

Let me tell you what happens to me. I was explaining something that happened with my daughters about a year ago. They were at a clothing store and a scumbag decided to try and intimidate them while they were standing by the register to pay. He, who stood at about six foot three, hovered within inches of them, both about five foot two. This clearly was intentional and made them extremely uncomfortable. When they came home and told me what had happened, anger bubbled up inside me.

When I shared this story a few days ago, I felt my body heating up again. My fists balled up and I found myself leaning forward and getting loud, though the people I was telling it to had absolutely nothing to do with the initial interaction. When I realized how worked up I was getting, merely by sharing the story, I had to take a deep breath and slow down. The friends I was talking to had both backed their chairs up. They said they could literally feel my rage over the situation and that it was so strong it had pushed them back. This jerk stimulated a reaction in me, and my energy had expanded exponentially, to the point that my friends felt overwhelmed by it. I had to reign my aura back in.

This energy, from our own aura, can be so powerful it can move people. Go back to how that angry memory or thought made you feel. What happened in that moment? Did you feel yourself getting larger? Or shrinking down? As I explained, just the thought of what the man had done to my kids triggered a reaction that increased my aura to create a formidable presence. Imagine what you could accomplish when you control that.

Let's look at it a different way, because we don't want to only work with our aura when we are angry. Let's imagine you are really happy! That's much better. Happy and excited even. Think back to a time when you felt that kind of feeling. What was it? Where were you? Did you feel warm or cold? How about your space—did you feel large? Or small? Did it feel like your energy was fluid with movement or stagnant and standing still? Think about this. Now really feel it. What does it feel like in your body? Does it make you feel good and tingly? Do you want to share that energy with others or hold it captive for yourself?

Everyone reacts differently to circumstances. You, and you alone, will feel how you react, and by extension, you will begin to feel how your energy and your aura react. But what about not waiting for a reaction to something? You've hopefully now experienced what your aura is capable of during extreme emotions. By focusing in on those feelings, you can train or learn to extend or retract your aura.

This, by the way, can be seen when viewed through an infrared camera. It's possible to physically see your auric energy expanding or retracting based on what you are feeling or who you are talking with. I've seen firsthand how an interesting conversation can alter the energy field around two people. When they first start to talk, their auras are held back, separate and independent of each other. But something incredible happens when they begin to get into what they are talking about, kind of like when you almost can't wait to chime in because you're so excited about the topic you're discussing. Their auras begin stretching out toward each other, and then *bam!* They merge together! The outer layers connect and form a big outline that encompasses both people, while their inner layers stay solely around each individual. Their auras link through their mutual excitement.

Why would you want to connect your aura with someone else's? Or reach your aura out toward them? Because you can! And because it can help you control and lead situations. There are so many practical reasons for this. If you are trying to bring someone around to your ideas or way of thinking, you need to connect to them. When you extend your aura out, they can join you, and it becomes much easier to sway your customer, client, or significant other to agree or understand your point of view.

## Try This!
## Focus on the Passion

Think of how you felt when you were angry. Now, think of how you felt when you were really happy, ecstatic even. Rather than focusing on the cause of the anger or happiness, instead focus on the passion. It is strong. It is powerful. That passion can be used to expand and control your auric field. When you breathe in, feel that passion filling your physical body. As you continue inhaling and allowing the passion to permeate inside you, begin letting it seep out through your pores. On every exhale, imagine that passion, that emotion you feel so strongly, is pushing out further and further until you get tingly. Now, and this is important, allow that energy to be positive and inviting instead of negative. Push your delight through your skin to your ethereal layers and feel what that does to your spirit.

When you expand your aura in this way, you are really doing double duty. You are not only magnifying your energy; you are also protecting yourself from other energy coming in to distract or interrupt yours. You're shielding negativity from getting through to interfere with your spirit. This, again, makes you powerful. Others will feel it and pull back their own energy without even realizing what they're doing, which can create a leadership spot for you. It opens up the perfect situation for you to exert your preferences and desires in business, and so on, to increase your potential for success.

Now that you know how it feels, how about another, easier way to increase your auric imprint? You can do this simply with your breath. Pretend you've drawn a circle around yourself, in the air. Yes, that takes some imagination on your part! Make it about five inches away from your physical body. Breathe. Just inhale and exhale. With every breath out, picture the space between your outline and your body filling with color, more specifically red, blue, and yellow. Red is a powerful color when envisioned with the intent of positive power rather than anger. Blue is about communication—listening as well as speaking. Yellow is your intuitive power center, where your gut instincts reside. When you keep breathing out and filling the void you've drawn with these colors, it will develop a much larger aura that others may begin to feel. You can utilize this method anywhere you need to feel more confident and stronger, raising you to greatness.

## Calming Your Nerves in an Unsteady World

We can internationally feel energy. There are so many stressors in our world, especially with all the crises that are happening globally. So how do these affect you? The truth is everything that's going on around you has the capacity to wear you down or boost you up. If the global predicaments aren't causing apprehension, think on a more personal level. In business, we tend to focus on what is happening externally, more than internally, and those events and circumstances affect us. We succumb to pressures from others at work, especially our bosses, based on what they are dealing with as their truth or their needs, because we want to empathize with them, but let's be real here—more so because we need to do what's necessary to stay employed. When we really take a moment to think about the situation or why we are doing the job we are doing, we can see that our truth may not align with theirs, and we may need to move on. But how can that ever happen if we don't take a minute to contemplate our options?

You've been working with your aura, and you know that through our energy, all living things are connected. This is why we can so easily be swayed or influenced by other people and the energy they put out in the world. Besides being sympathetic to others, we can also be empathetic and even empathic. *Empathic* means we feel what other people are feeling. This can cause us to start freaking out for no reason. You may begin to feel sad or uncomfortable when the world seems to be having so many problems. You pick up on the energy with clairsentience. Good, bad, or indifferent, it's all there, and you need to learn how to separate the energy that's not yours. Empaths want the world to live in harmony—their desire for peace comes from their deep connection to so many. When you take on energy that doesn't belong to you, it's much better when it's positive energy. While this may be true, you have to be prepared for anything.

Don't be afraid of your energy. Be grateful, but don't be naïve and think that everyone will have the same feelings or vibes as you. They won't always be able to calm down, but you will! Take a deep breath. You want to be able to pull your own energy back in so you can control it a bit better. Now, here's the thing: you don't necessarily always want to completely sever your energy to and from others. You want to stay connected and tapped into what's happening in the world and in your own little portion of it. You don't want to let it overtake you, though. Instead of totally cutting the threads between you and the rest of society, imagine that what connects you is like an electrical cord, and you are in control of it and can settle it down when needed.

Electrical cords have many wires woven together to make up the actual cable. It is these wires that carry the energy from one point or connection to the other. Similar to this, imagine a bunch of multiwired cables connecting you to the world and everyone in it. Rather than envisioning yourself cutting the entire thing and amputating your link, start slowly by imagining yourself severing one wire at a time.

There are some contacts we need to keep undamaged, like those to our boss or our employee or customer. However, there's nothing that says we need to keep the flow wide open. By decreasing the number of wires in each cable that attaches you to each particular person, you can get rid of some of the stress that weighs you down, leaving only the positive or necessary filaments. This will help you understand each other and what you need to do, while keeping your own personal space and boundaries intact. You've got this. You can handle it, deliberately and with intent. At first, it may feel exhausting, especially if you don't know which links to cut to each person or situation, but with practice and focus you will learn to accomplish this with little effort.

Now, remember—we all have situations or people who stress us out. Send yourself some positive energy. Give yourself a break. It's all right to stress. It's what you do with it that will determine whether you use the energy all around you or let it use and drain you. Further, when you become more adept at managing the stressors, you will have more of an opportunity to examine your options. Should you expand your energy? Should you retract it? Should you cut the entire bundled cord to someone or something or pick and choose which individual wires to cut? Whether it is personal or business, you need to be able to examine these choices if you want to get ahead, even with the static that is constantly buzzing. And then, you will succeed.

## Calming Down
## in the Midst of Chaos

When was the last time you felt really calm? When you were working on a big pitch at work? When you were dealing with employee issues? When you were trying to handle your two teenage kids at home who just told you that one wanted to drop out of school and the other one was pregnant? Ha. That's real life, though. Not everyone's daily life is going to be the same, and not everyone will deal with these types of stress, but we've all got some form of chaos in our life that needs to be dealt with. The only way to handle serious issues is to rationally approach them individually. But how can you be a success if you're not conquering everything at once? Well, you can and then some. And you can start this by meditating. You need to calm down.

You've pulled your energy back. You've cut whatever cords necessary to be able to move on, but now what do you do? You meditate. You relax your mind, body, and spirit. If you don't, you can suffer from overload. Meditation can bring about a total relaxation that can leave you ready to handle just about anything. There are many ways to begin and many ways to direct your meditation. Meditation can bring about positivity and chase away negative feelings. Among other benefits, it can increase the productivity as well as boost the brain's ability to process information. Of course, this will add to your quality of life.

It's interesting—when you look up *meditation* in a thesaurus, it throws out words like *consideration*, *contemplation*, and *introspection*. You are concentrating on your mind and even changing your mindset. You are relaxing your thoughts, decreasing the stress, and increasing your body's actual comfort. Your spirit is longing for this, and you're going to provide it!

### *Try This!*
### Meditate Using Your Breath

The most basic of meditations can be accomplished by breathwork, which can be extremely effective. Focusing on both the inhalation and the exhalation while counting to three or four is the simplest way to begin. If you do this for a mere five minutes a day, you will find yourself becoming calmer. Again, calming down is so important to your successes in both your personal and professional life. When you inhale, imagine a beautiful, loving energy entering your lungs and spreading through your body. As you exhale, feel any gunk or negativity pass out through your mouth, ridding your mind, body, and spirit of anything that's not yours to hold on to or anything you no longer need. Then, and this is a biggie, thank the universe for holding space for you to relax in this hectic world.

The more you practice this simple meditation, the more natural it will begin to feel. When you are ready to progress to the next level, you can still begin in this way, but do it with purpose. Go somewhere you will be comfortable and can sit or lie down for a longer period of time—whether it's your own bed or your office is irrelevant as long as you won't be disturbed. The next step in your meditation practice (and I say practice because it's a never-ending development) is to set an intention. Think about what it is you want to accomplish today, this week, this month, this year. Set a goal. It might be to increase your business portfolio or your business network, or it may have more to do with losing the extra weight you've put on due to stress. Whatever your goal, this meditative exercise can help you achieve it.

Think about what your goal is and get comfortable. It's imperative that you are comfy to help with your attention. You can begin with the simple breathwork. Once you've gotten yourself to a place where you feel relaxed and are ready to work on your goals, you'll know. It's okay if you feel distracted—we all get distracted. Just acknowledge whatever random thoughts you have, thank them for showing up, and let them go. Get back to the business at hand. When you feel inclined to continue, it's the right time. Then, with every inhalation, breathe in your goal. Taste it, feel it, see it, inhale it, say it in your mind. With every outward breath, rid your mental state of the obstacles and debris you've been holding on to that have held you back from accomplishing what you want. See the obstacles, visualize what they are, and watch them funnel out of your mouth. Be sure to include yourself in there—most often it's us that hold ourselves back. Don't stop until you feel you're done. And, as always, thank the universe for having your back and for allowing you to make these changes.

Do this work every day for at least a week and pay attention to how you feel. Has your overall energy changed? Do you find yourself more relaxed? Have you calmed down? If so, great! If you don't feel a difference yet, then keep doing it. Giving up is no longer in your vocabulary. You are worth more than that, and it's about time you realized it. Remember, you are powerful, and it's up to you to start owning that!

Energy is a mighty tool when utilized. Discovering how we can connect and control and even manipulate the energy to our benefit or the benefit of others can give you a leg up over your competition. The energy of your aura will serve you well and can even boost your ability to manifest the life you want to live.

# CHAPTER 6
# Manifesting

*When you know your highest self, you are on your way*
*to becoming a co-creator of your entire world, learning to manage*
*the circumstances of your life and participating with assurance*
*in the act of creation. You literally become a manifester.*

—DR. WAYNE DYER

I'm often asked what manifesting is exactly and if it's real. Here is the low-down on manifesting: *we create what we think about.* This simply means we can bring about good or bad things in our life. If we constantly think about how our boss is going to give us the shittiest jobs, they probably will. Contrary to the negative, if we visualize and see ourselves receiving tasks we enjoy or the types of responsibilities we want to handle, we can create that reality instead. Believing it is possible to manifest what you want is key to actually manifesting what you want. Manifestation, at its core, is the creation of something out of nothing or creating that which we give energy to, and, yes, it's for real.

Here's the question: Exactly what can you manifest? Well, pretty much anything. Need a new partner? Manifest it. Need a new job? Manifest it. Need a new car? Manifest it. Need a new home? Manifest that too. Having said this, it doesn't mean it's instant. And it doesn't mean it's always going to happen.

What I've discovered is it may take quite a bit of time. It also has to be for our greater good. What does that suggest? Essentially, if it is beneficial to our life's path, and if it is in line with our lessons, then what we are asking for may come to fruition. If not, it probably won't.

This can sound a little complicated, so let's look at it from this perspective. Pretend you decide you want to manifest being a movie star, out of the blue. Sounds great, right? However, what if you graduated with a law degree and are about to help people who otherwise wouldn't receive the assistance they need? Now, I am not saying you give up your dream for someone else's. Rather, I suggest you think about whether you'd feel fulfilled in your life with either path. The universe needs all types of people to keep flowing energetically, and for the most part we have freedom of choice, but there is also a reason each and every one of us is here. If being a movie star doesn't align with your energy, you probably won't manifest it. Alternatively, if you barely made it through law school and felt a deep pull toward Hollywood your entire life, then there's a pretty high probability that being on the big screen is more lined up with your destiny.

Understanding what it is we want is usually the first step in manifesting anything. Everyone has their own thing; no two people are the same or want exactly the same things. At any given point in your life your desires will change. What you want can rapidly transform into something entirely different. This should not preclude you from attempting to manifest along the way, though. There are no rules that say you have to manifest only big, life-changing things. You can work on the smaller affairs along the way. Your needs may shift yearly, monthly, weekly, or even daily. It is possible to focus on the little things while you are still trying to figure out what your wishes are for the long term. The good thing about manifestation is it can help you get what you lack in all areas of your life.

## How to Manifest Money Using Your Intuition

We all want money and that's not a bad thing. Money for money's sake is nothing too special. But what money can do for us or what we can do with it—now that is what makes it amazing. Money does not equate to success, however. It's what having money represents and the power it can bring that people equate with it. So let's make some money!

Money comes to us in so many different ways and from so many different sources. When we manifest it, we want to be sure that it flows from a place that doesn't hurt anyone else or create problems for anyone else. We won't *always* know how the money will come to be, but sometimes we do. Here's an example. One of the most common frustrations is when money comes through an inheritance. It's one thing if it's from your great-grandmother who was 100 years old and lived a fabulous life and was ready to go. It's quite another when your fifty-eight-year-old parent passes unexpectedly, leaving you a decent bank account. Obviously, we don't want someone to have to die to bring our manifestations to fruition, but for sure be open to manifestation happening in a variety of ways.

Years ago, after I spent way too much on Christmas, I needed to manifest some cash flow. I asked that it hurt no one but that it would come quickly. Sure enough, the next day, my husband and I came home to a busted water heater. Now, immediately I had the negative thoughts—my basement was flooded. My house was going to be ruined. This, added on to already being stretched thin, almost put me over the edge. Until I realized what had happened.

Turns out, there was no lasting damage at all. We called our insurance company and they sent someone out right away, the next day in fact. On top of that, they actually cut us a check for thousands of dollars on the spot. Never in a million years would I have believed that would have happened or that my request to manifest money would have been fulfilled in that way or that quickly.

Believing you can manifest what you want is crucial. So what do you want? What are you hoping for? How much money is enough? What do you want it for? Do you have bills to pay? Do you need a new washing machine? You can start by creating what you need first.

When you achieve those smaller things first, it will give you confidence to go for the big asks.

 ### *Try This!*
### Manifest

Focus in on what you want—whether it's a specific dollar amount for something or just a little extra spending money is totally up to you. Write it down. Be precise. If you want $100, then write $100. If you want money so you can buy a cup of coffee everyday instead of having to make it, write down how much that would be. If you want to take a trip to the Caribbean, figure out what that will cost, and write that amount down. It's up to you to know exactly how much you are requesting from the universe.

Then ask for it. Ask the universe to provide you with that specified amount. Along with the amount, set a time frame. Don't just say "right now." Be logical. It's one thing to say money will fall from the heavens and quite another to think it will happen as you are reading this book. Let's not get too crazy. Be reasonable but state a time frame that will work for you and not cause any undue stress by having to wait too long, especially if it is money you need to pay the rent. Then add that to your dollar amount on your paper.

Once you've figured all of that out, you need to thank the universe. I know, I know—you haven't gotten anything yet. Your expectation and your gratitude are needed to help your manifestation along. Do you think you'll get everything you want without being gracious? Very rarely will that happen, and even then there will be an eventual price to pay. On top of thanking the universe for essentially granting your wish, thank it for doing so in a healthy, nonlethal, legal way. Uh-huh, legal. You don't want something falling into your lap that you'll later get arrested for, and as I said, you don't want anyone to get hurt or even die for you to get your money, unless it is indeed their time to go.

In order to be thankful, you have to be sure to believe. It can be crazy difficult sometimes to believe that you will be able to effectively create money out of nothing. That is what you're doing. Remember, though, that it's not you—it's the universe, God, your deceased loved ones, and even your guides that are making this happen for you.

(Whatever your beliefs are, I usually lump it all together and call it the universe!) You are requesting help and you are worthy of it. Imagine you need money to buy a suit so you can go on a job interview so you can make enough money to pay for a place to live for you and your baby. That is something that, for sure, is worth it. The energy of the universe will provide for you. Believe that. How can you even begin to be a formidable force if you can't believe there is more to life than what you currently hold in your pocket?

Now, and this is usually the hardest part of manifesting, let it go. Give it up to the universe to make it happen. You've requested a specific dollar amount within a specified time frame, hopefully to no one's detriment. You've been *extremely* grateful, and you believe it will happen. What is better than that? All that's left now is to wait. Stop thinking about it. Know that help is on the way and your prayers will be answered. You've made it happen. You are, after all, worthy.

Okay, okay. I just told you to let it go, right? This is going to sound contradictory. You need to let it go, but—and this is a big but—you need to be present in your life! I am not telling you to focus all your attention on making your manifestation happen. You shouldn't. What you need to do, though, is participate in your life. You can't ignore the phenomena that you are presented with. There very well may be mechanisms at work that will show up for you. Don't disregard them. I'm talking about the stuff that drops in your lap, that comes out of nowhere.

When you manifest, be aware of things that pop up that may assist in making your wishes materialize. If you are asking for more money to come in and then you're offered a new job with an increased salary, this may be just what you're looking for. If you want more time to write the great American novel and your hours get cut down at your job, consider this a segue into becoming the author of that book. If you are trying to manifest a new relationship and your friend calls to set you up on a blind date, go! All these things are happening to help you manifest what you want. Consider the new job with the increased salary, be thankful for having your hours reduced, put on your best outfit, and go on that get-together! These opportunities are the universe's way of bringing about what you are trying to receive. Pay attention and be present in your own life.

## Ask for What You Really Want

You've just started manifesting, using a defined amount of money for something you need or want. But if you could ask for any amount of money, what would it be? I was teaching a class recently and asked the question, "How much money would you manifest?" The answers varied. Some stated they were asking for just enough to pay their bills for the month, and others wanted to manifest a couple hundred thousand dollars. I had a few who decided two million was a nice round number. And finally, Nelly said ten million. When people questioned her, Nelly replied, "Well, why the hell *wouldn't* I ask for ten?" It made the entire class question their own requests.

How much is enough? If you need a raise at work, is a quarter enough? Should that be all you ask for, or should you ask for more? When you want to get ahead in business, you need to believe it is possible and that you are worth it. Manifesting should be realistic, but you needn't hesitate to go after what you want. How much is actually enough? The answer is simple—what you will settle for is enough, because that's all you are willing to manifest. Are you limiting what you are manifesting because you don't believe you deserve more, need more, or will get more?

I am with Nelly—ask for it all! Start manifesting it. Your thoughts will direct what you receive. Reach for the stars, right?

When we are young, we are told we can be anything, do anything, and have anything we want. Why, as adults, do we begin limiting ourselves? Why, when we can manifest virtually anything, would we put a cap on it? Possibly more to the point, who decides what that cap is? It's on you, in essence, to decide what is enough for you. Only you can determine what you deserve. Believing all you'll get is a quarter is exceptionally self-restrictive. You are curbing the universe's desire to help you out before it's even allowed to begin.

You, probably unintentionally, put constraints on what you're worth. Maybe it's because you don't feel you deserve it, or it may simply be that you're too polite to want more. But, come on, in order to succeed, you need to have a sense of self-worth; otherwise, it is like a complete contradiction.

It is up to you to set the boundaries of what you desire. It is on you to determine how much or how little is enough. Don't listen to your friend Madge, who tells you it's bullshit and you have to work really hard to get money. Don't listen to your last bad relationship when your partner told you that you would never have anything because you're not worth it. And, definitely, without a doubt, don't listen to anyone who tells you that you don't deserve it. Instead, listen to me, an absolute stranger, who can tell you with complete and utmost certainty, that you are, without a doubt, deserving and worthy of every dime you are trying to manifest.

Steve Jobs, creator of Apple and other companies, knew about manifestation. He said, "Don't let the noise of others' opinions drown out your own inner voice. And most important, have the courage to follow your heart and intuition. They somehow already know what you truly want to become. Everything else is secondary."[8] Take that, naysayers! It is the truth, and you will be laughing all the way to the bank.

Manifesting money is really the beginning—there is so much more you can focus on. Imagine seeing a car that you really want. Maybe it's a sleek sportscar, low stance, clean, sharp lines. You can see the color, silver, which conjures up thoughts of a silver bullet. Because of this imagery, you just know this car is fast, and that's exactly what you want. The inside has to be just as cool as the outside, right? There is a leather interior, and it's probably a six-speed, because even if you don't already know how to drive stick, you'd learn for this car. It's got a back seat, but that's mostly just for show—no normal-size legs would fit back there—and the steering wheel is the perfect shape and size for your hands. This is your perfect car. You've just focused on the details of your car (well, okay, my car).

8. Steve Jobs, Stanford University Commencement Address, June 12, 2005, https://news
.stanford.edu/2005/06/14/jobs-061505/.

Take advantage of manifestation for business. You can manifest what you want by tuning in to your intuition. Use your clairvoyance to look ahead and see what would happen if you were successful. Use clairaudience to ask for some instruction on what best suits you. Possibly more prevalently, use clairsentience to help you tune in to how your business ideas feel to you. Often times what happens is you've gotten stuck trying to see past the brick wall you've constructed on your path. You can just go around it instead of trying to force your way through it. In other words, you can do it the hard way and bang your head against the wall or do it the easy way by manifesting.

## Try This!
## Vision Board to Focus
## Your Energy on What You Want

Much the same way we visualized my car, you can visualize a new business and use that to manifest it. We visualize what we want in great detail, and, actually, we can create our vision externally, not just in our imagination, by making a vision board. A *vision board* is a compilation of images from magazines, pictures, or drawings. Anything that assembles your wishes, hopes, and desires can serve as your vision board. For example, if you want to create a vision board for the upcoming year, you may include pictures of beaches or foreign lands, books, wedding dresses, and money. These may represent your desire to travel, relax, read or write, find a significant other to marry, and make lots of money. (It's been my experience that money is pretty much always on everyone's vision board in one way or another!) Your vision board can include everything you want to manifest, including a new business, and is the best way to really take it from your imagination to a more physical level, something you can look at in great detail.

Often, people find it easier to "create" rather than simply ask for something. By making a vision board, you have something tangible you can hold on to. You have given a great deal of thought to what you want and are putting it out there for the world to see. More so, you've gathered together a multitude of wishes all in one space, and it's something you can easily look at.

By collecting all of it onto your board, you are in a way explaining to the universe just about everything you want to create over the next twelve months or so. I usually make vision boards around the turn of the new year with the expectation that what I desire will come to be at some point during that time frame. Nine times out of ten I won't get everything because I have a lot on my board, but the mere act of conceptualizing this and putting it out there opens me to the infinite possibilities of getting what I want. You can do the same. Don't be surprised that you don't get everything. Think about it this way. If you have a myriad of wants and desires, you are not focusing all your attention on everything. More likely, you've chosen one or two things that are important, and the universe can feel that.

Regardless of the time of year, go ahead and assemble your own vision board. Gather a bunch of old magazines and pictures. Get some leftover craft supplies from your kids' last project. Collect your markers and crayons. Have some glitter and ribbon on standby as well. There is no limit to what you can use to put your vision board together.

There are basically two different ways to construct your manifestation piece. The first is to know exactly what you want on your board and go through your supplies to find pictures or stuff to represent it on your board. The second is to start looking through the magazines and see what strikes your fancy. What jumps out at you? Both methods work equally well, and I recommend combining the two. You generally know what you want, so searching through everything to find it is a great way to start. Then, looking through the stuff with no specific direction can open you up to ideas or things you may not have even realized you wanted or may have overlooked.

For example, I am an author—I know, it's redundant to state but significant. I didn't think about putting books on my last vision board until I saw a picture of a pile of books. That got me thinking—how many more books, if any, did I want to write? It did get my juices flowing and opened me up to the possibility that I would conceivably write more!

How about you? What do you want on your vision board? Is it money? Is it a new job? How about that new car? What about landing that new deal? Or a trip to Greece? Gather different representations of possible business ventures you're thinking of establishing. You can even reinvent yourself on your board to be the person you desperately want to be. The sky is the virtual limit. There is no holding you back now.

Use symbolism as well. Imagine Steve Jobs making a vision board so many years ago with only an apple on it. Wow, how powerful that can be. Use symbols to represent what you want to pull into your life and what's important to you currently as well as in the future. Only you know what that may be and what is good for you. If you are trying to move up in your company, think about what that would look like symbolically, and then put that on your vision board. Determining that you want to travel more, and do it in first class, can also be represented on your display through symbolism. If you want to speak to large audiences, possibly a big microphone is what needs to be part of your vision. If you want to run a company with a lot of employees, maybe you can paste on images of minions. The only boundaries you have when creating your very own personal vision board is the amount of stuff you can actually fit on it.

Whether you are manifesting in your personal life or you are doing it for your professional achievements, you've just absorbed many ways to create a life you'll love. If you are looking for 100 percent security and absolute gains, taking advantage of your ability to manifest will help you on your way. What can be better than creating something from nothing? That's manifestation at its core. After you begin using these methods, you will instantly benefit.

There is nothing wrong with using every possible means you can to build a life you want and expecting that you absolutely can! Positive manifestation can only happen when you don't block it. Fundamentally, we as humans are not flawless, nor are we flawed, though sometimes we have a tendency to hinder our own progress. We are learning how to work with our energy to create our best possible outcome in every situation. We have to step out of our comfort zone to reach those outcomes and take risks, but not without checking in with our vibes.

CHAPTER 7

# Minimizing Fallout
# from Risks, Self-Sabotage,
# and Procrastination

*When people allow instinct and intuition to be part*
*of their decision-making process, they experience less regret*
*and feel less conflicted when they make important decisions.*

—KAROL WARD

There is an excitement to taking a chance, to stepping into the unknown or trying something that could be slightly dangerous. Knowing that you won't ever get ahead unless you try something new can be very compelling. Getting that rush, that feeling of accomplishment when the risk you are taking was somehow successful, can make it worth the danger. But taking chances inherently increases risk. When you go out on a limb, that limb can break, creating chaos instead of perceived order. Your intuition can help narrow down which actions you should take, lessening the risks.

If we didn't ever have to take a chance or if we don't have to work for it in some way, what good is the reward? We might as well sit on our hands, and what fun would that be? Taking risks to better yourself and those around you can be priceless, depending on what you're doing. Frequently, we take more risks in our personal lives than we do in business because we are so afraid of losing our job, our client, our position, and even our significance if we take a risk and fail. This is understandable when you have people depending on you, including yourself. It can be very scary.

Look beyond the risk to the quality of life. Being driven often comes at a price. You won't win every time, but you won't win anytime if you don't try. If you start looking at successful people, the interesting thing is that they are always moving forward. They've gotten to the point where they don't have to question whether it's worth it or not. They just trust it will work out and dive in. They've determined through experience that there will always be risk and they take the risks that feel right. More often than not it is worth the reward because of the way it's worked out previously. They believe it will turn out to be positive, so they are confident. The universe makes it happen. They are optimists living with the expectation that all will be good. They trust their intuition and operate on the assumption that it will be a success, which, in their eyes, minimizes the risk. But there's a good possibility it wasn't always that way.

Once they started taking risks and realizing that things wouldn't change unless they took some intuitively directed chances, their mindset changed, and they began transforming their lives. The thought of self-sabotage isn't part of their mentality. Now, they dive in without hesitation once they determine it is something they want. They don't procrastinate.

When you live with a poverty consciousness instead, you tend to question and doubt whether the risks are worth it. If you've grown up with scarcity, you are used to scarcity and therefore have a difficult time taking the chance. This generally holds true in your professional and personal life. Taking a risk with a relationship can be more daunting if you were raised without a father or mother because he or she took off and left you to be cared for by your single mom or dad. Never having the money to pay the rent during childhood has become your (unintended) mantra, and it's always a struggle, so taking a chance and possibly losing your job can be terrifying. These are real concerns and real fears. These are not unique in general but are very specific to each individual. Like the people mentioned earlier who were able to use their intuition to minimize fallout, who were able to change their mindset, you have to decide if you're ready to start taking risks—even if you begin with small ones.

### *Try This!*
### Why Not Take the Risk?

Think of what holds you back. Think of why you may not want to take risks. Could it be because you don't believe you can do it? Is it because you've had so many bad experiences already that you don't think it's possible for you to have good ones? Is it because you've failed multiple times in the past, so you take it for granted that's what it will always be? Could it be because you feel like you don't deserve it? Is it a poverty consciousness or something else you grew up with that has taught you things won't work out?

These are all valid reasons. However, taking the risk may very well be exactly what you need in order to move forward. But you shouldn't do it blindly. Instead, let's practice.

Think of something you want but you need to take a risk in order to get. It could be a new job, a relocation, a raise, and so on. Focus in on what it is. Think about what the actual risks would be. Now, tune in to your intuition. If you were to take the risk, what do your intuitive vibes tell you?

- You will fail.
- You will succeed.
- It's a good idea.
- It may not produce the outcome you expected.
- It will be better than you expected.
- You will be happy.
- You will be miserable.
- You will feel like you accomplished something great.

- It will be a step back in your career or life.
- It will propel you to the next level in your career or life.

Once you've gone through all the possible outcomes and more, using your intuition, think about how it felt, what you saw in your mind's eye, and if you heard anything or just knew things about taking the risk. Going even deeper, did your intuitive senses match, or did they give you different answers? If they were different, focus in again using all your psychic gifts and determine, kind of by unanimous decision, which way you are leaning. Remember, you can always ask your intuition for clarity if you're not sure what it's trying to convey to you.

You can use this type of guidance anytime you are debating whether to take any size risk, whether it is big or small, with a caveat that you try to follow through with what your intuitive guidance is telling you! Taking that risk may be exactly what you need to jump-start your success.

## No Regrets

Think of it as risk versus reward. If you take the chance, you may be rewarded. If you don't, you'll never know what the reward would have been. I am not saying every risk is worth the chance of reward, but if you let your fear control your actions, you will stay stuck exactly where you are. You won't ever be able to get ahead in business or in life. You will be stagnant. Everyone knows, in theory, that you only regret the chances you didn't take. But we are talking reality here, and the reality is you may regret chances you took that didn't work out. When you take a chance and it doesn't work out, it can make you or break you, which is why it is so important to check in with your intuition before jumping headlong into something blindly. However, if you don't use your intuition or take any chances, you never know what will actually work out. The fear of failure will inevitably create regrets in every part of your life.

I worked with a client, Daniel, who played sports. In Daniel's first year, he played well only until someone else bested him, and he then shrank back and took on a supporting role. When he came to me, questioning why he wasn't scoring anymore, I told him, "You will remember playing. You may remember some of your teammates. You won't remember the goals you missed. You damn sure will remember the goals you made! So take the initiative and go for it!" Just like Daniel, when you begin doubting your abilities or you let someone else's expertise overshadow yours, you allow yourself to fail. Failing is easy; everyone can do it. The real challenge is to go for it—give it 110 percent, knowing that even if you fail, you won't regret it because at least you are moving toward your goals. Fight for what you want! Go after what you desire by making those moves, and you won't be disappointed.

## An Open Mind and a Willingness to Succeed Are All You Need

It is amazing when you begin connecting to your intuition—you start to feel a bit less vulnerable and less exposed because you can be more confident in what you are doing. At this point, whether you have a highly developed business acumen or you're still in the embryonic stage is irrelevant. All you really need is the desire for greatness. Expect success now. You've activated your metaphysical senses and by combining them with your existing skills, there will be no stopping your growth. Staying open to the process will automatically propel you forward and keep you on your path to becoming the badass you want to be.

When you use your intuition to help guide you with your decision-making, you lessen the risk of the action you are taking. If you knew what the outcome would be before you jumped into something, it would make you so much more secure. You'd feel comforted in the wisdom that what you are going to do will have a positive outcome. Clearly, this would lessen your fear and make it more feasible to attempt things. Anything becomes easy when you know the end result ahead of time.

Making smart decisions will always be better than diving headlong into new experiences blindly. Remember in chapter 1 when I defined your basic clair senses—clairvoyance (sight), clairaudience (hearing), clairsentience (feeling), and claircognizance (knowing)? These are the senses you need to use in order to tune in to any given situation. Utilizing your intuitive abilities will help you lessen any risks and increase all your gains. You can start with a very basic intuitive feedback system and progress to a more highly developed intuitive guidance technique as you increase your acumen.

Think about betting on the roulette wheel. When you place a color bet, meaning you choose not a number but either black or red, you have a fifty-fifty chance of doubling your money. There are basically two ways to decide the bet. The first is to guess. Literally, just guess. Your odds are still fifty-fifty. Or you can use your gut. You know this to be your intuition and, more specifically, your clairsentience. Placing your bet by feeling if you put it on the right color may increase your odds of winning. Why not do this with every risk you take in life?

Raising your awareness also raises your probability of success. I don't claim you will be right all the time. You will get better as you go. Think about what risk is involved. If it's monetary, it could be as small as one dollar or infinitely bigger. When you become more comfortable with your intuitive feelings, you will find you will take bigger chances. Whether at the casino or in your business, you have to raise the stakes a bit, and that works much better if you have greater insight into what your better options may be.

Risk does not always involve money, but let's start there, because we can all use a little more. When all is said and done, money can't buy happiness, but it can definitely make it easier to be happy. Using your clairsentience, you might find you can decrease your risk, and you might be surprised at how attainable your goals can be. Having said that, let's do some work to help you realize how it can work for you.

### Try This!
### Pick a Stock, Any Stock

Go ahead and open a newspaper and go to the stocks area. If you don't have a newspaper, you can go online and find a stock site. Pick out five stocks that you see, preferably ones that you are not familiar with or that you know nothing about. You are going to become a market aficionado and intuit the trend for each stock over the next week or so. Write down the first stock in the middle of a piece of paper. Put it in front of you.

To really tune in to your intuitive vibes, you must relax. In order to do that, you can work on your meditative breathing for a few minutes. Once you feel your mind, body, and spirit slowing down, start meditating on that particular stock. Breathe in and out, thinking of the stock the whole time. See the actual name of the stock or the stock symbol in your mind. Ask, internally or out loud, which direction you feel the stock moving. You might feel a slight tug one way or the other. Pay attention if your body or even just one part of you, like your head or your arm, feels pulled. Notice if your body temperature changes or gets cooler or even warmer on one side versus the other. One side of you may twitch a bit; feel that. How does it feel in your gut? What's your knee-jerk reaction? Usually, that's an indication of your clear sensing drawing you toward something. In this case, your intuition will be letting you know whether this particular stock is moving you down or up. Now, flip over your paper, and based on what you felt, draw an arrow up or down to represent the stock's price either increasing or decreasing over the next day. Write the date next to the arrow on the back of the paper.

After you've done this for the first stock, do the same for each of the others, one at a time. When you do the second stock, it might actually feel different than it did with the first one. This may be due to the direction of the stock's trajectory (gaining or losing value), or it might be because it is a more familiar exercise the second time around. If it didn't feel like you were lured either way for any of them, that's okay. Just go ahead and guess. Usually our best guesses, especially after meditation, have a basis in intuition, even if we don't recognize it as such.

When you've worked all the stocks, put away the papers. Don't look at them, don't compare your answers, and above all, don't judge the work you did. Over the next week or so, do it again, each day, recording your projections for the week. Don't look at what you've already intuited every day until after you do the work. Then, flip the paper again and write the date and direction you felt drawn to.

At the end of the week, pull out the newspapers for each day or open each stock on the internet on a site that will show you the daily stock value. Record the starting value on the first day, and then mark the values for each date that you tuned in. Compare the actual activity to what you recorded. Pay special attention to any trends you notice. In particular, you may have been right on with one stock and not so much with another.

Beyond whether you were right or wrong, how did it feel? Did you gain confidence in your clairsentience the more you used it, or did it stress you out? Did you enjoy it? Was it comfortable? Was it hard not looking right away to see if you were right? And were you right, for the most part, or wrong? If you were wrong every single time, maybe it's because you misread your body's clues. For example, now you know that if you feel cold on the left, that means to going up instead of down and vice versa.

This method of risk can be simply vetted by doing exercises like the stock predictions. Not only will it help you practice tuning in, but it also has great potential to help you make some money in the market. Don't forget, actually playing in the stock exchange never comes with guarantees, so be smart and know when it feels right or when it feels wrong. Start small until you feel comfortable. Then you can wager more money, and yes, you bet I said "wager" because there is definitely risk involved. Be that speculator and work it—with a decreased risk when you listen to what your intuition is telling you.

## Visualize Risk Reduction

You've just utilized your clairsentience, along with a smattering of your other senses. Concentrating on your clairvoyance can present you with another way to tune in to your intuition to reduce risk. Seeing possible outcomes in your mind's eye can lead to a deeper understanding of what you should do in a particular situation. If you have the knowledge to make better choices, why wouldn't you use it? If you could see which side of the coin was going to land face up before it flipped, wouldn't you pick it? Just think of the possibilities.

Make your life easier—trust your intuition to help you however you can. In order to do that clairvoyantly, you can use symbolism to assist you in perceiving what your intuitive guidance system is trying to impart to you. Symbols offer you a way to interpret the impressions you get when you tune in.

Imagine, if you will, that you have decided to make a change at work. There's no urgency, so it's on you to settle on what time of year you should aim for to switch it up. How can you select the best month or season? You can just throw caution to the wind and not tap into your natural gifts. You've got a 25 percent chance that it would be the optimal plan. Or you can utilize your clear sight, reducing your risk of making a move at the wrong time. Let's do it that way.

### Try This!
### What Do You Want Out of Work?

Employing your past practice of breathing and meditation from chapter 4, go ahead and let yourself relax a bit before trying to tap in. Once you've chilled out, think about what you want to accomplish by shifting your job. Do you want to leave where you are working altogether? Do you want to switch up your own inventory? Do you want to run a sale special? Are you hoping to get a raise or a promotion that you need to apply for? Do you need to hire someone to help with your responsibilities? Decide what it is you are hoping to attain.

Now that you've established what you want to do, it's time to do the work. You are going to allow your intuition to show you, clairvoyantly, when would be best for you to make the changes you are looking forward to. Close your eyes and think of the seasons, using symbols to represent each one. For example, you may see a strawberry for summer, a pinecone for winter, a pumpkin for fall, and a flower for spring. Using these examples gives you a quick, more complete answer. Now, see yourself, in your imagination, in your new position, career, or job. Where are you and what are you doing? Without censoring or judgment, ask for one of the season symbols to show up in your mind's eye to let you know in what season you've successfully made the change. Does it make sense? Did you see the image clearly? Did you see something else?

When you've finished, do it again. Come at it from a different angle. This will help you establish if what you're visualizing is truly your clairvoyance at work or something else. It can be difficult to know whether your imagination has taken over, but double-checking helps. As with all your gifts, the more you practice the more you'll be able to validate what you are getting intuitively. By practicing using your basic gifts on a somewhat regular basis, you will become more confident.

The wisdom you've gained by visually intuiting the symbol to show you the best time to make your move will afford you the greatest possible outcome. Maybe you would be fine if you changed things up during any season, but things may not work out if you did it at the wrong time. This is about reducing the risk you are taking by tuning in. By seeing with your intuition, you can have faith that you've picked the right period in your life to switch it up. You're not only lowering the risks; you're upping your potential gains. What could be better than that?

Obviously, you can use this method of using symbols to look ahead clairvoyantly for any area of your life: when or with whom to list your house, when to move across country, which job to take, which job to apply for, whom to hire, whom to fire, and so on. Essentially, when you need to evaluate your choices, tap into your intuitive sight to reduce the risks of ending up with a bad result by seeing the better ones in your mind's eye.

## Try This!
## Listen Up to Reduce Risk

Imagine that you have a huge presentation to do. Maybe it's to your board members at work or it's to try and land a new account with a potential client. Here's the rub: if you blow this, your job is toast. You'll have to pack your bags and walk out with your tail between your legs. This production of yours will have to be spot on. What you choose to do for the actual presentation can make you or break you. How can you reduce the risk of flushing your career down the toilet? You listen with your clairaudience.

It's critical to figure out ahead of time what they will be looking for. What will excite your superiors or your newest customers? If you don't settle on a specific theme or option they will appreciate, you are risking just about everything. Like before, you can guess. By guessing you are using a bit of intuitive juice already, mixed with logic based on what you know about the people you're presenting to. When you specifically tap into your psychic abilities, though, you increase your odds of producing the best performance they'll want to see.

Let's suppose you can either pitch them product X or product Y, which, to your knowledge, are both good. But they have a lot of options available with other people, so you need to make sure you have the one they are more interested in pursuing. How can you accomplish that? By utilizing your clairaudient gift. Listening with your intuition can tell you exactly which direction to go in to lessen the chance they will fire you.

Focus in on your intuitive hearing. What might you hear that would indicate an answer in the affirmative? What sound would indicate a negative? For example, you might hear a *ding, ding, ding* to let you know that's a good idea, or a song that plays in your head with the lyrics "no, no, no, no, no." You might hear the actual word for which thing is the right thing for your particular situation. There are so many ways to tune in to your clairaudience that you are bound to find one that will resonate with you more, and that may become your easiest, go-to way to help you manage risks.

Relax using your meditative methods. Breathe until you feel grounded. Think about products one at a time. See them in your mind's eye next to each other—product X and product Y. When you've gotten to a good place and can see the products, imagine turning up the volume on your new internal earbuds. Adjust both sides equally;

this way you will hear with both ears internally. You've got the sound up perfectly, so let's do this. Visualize product X. What do you hear? Any sounds, songs, words? Pay attention to whether they seem to be in the affirmative or the negative. If you're not sure, ask for another sound to confirm. When you've gotten your answer(s), immediately change gears and focus on product Y and do the same thing. Do you get more of a positive vibe from one versus the other? More of a negative sense?

If you can't hear anything, it may simply be because you can't relate to this situation. Remember, you can adapt this exercise to something that's more personal to you. Try using these methods, all your intuitive gifts, for a condition in your life that you need help with. You will likely find it will work better for you! Your clairaudience is waiting to be heard!

## Knowing How to Lessen the Risk

You've already used your other clair senses to help you reduce risks, but what if you just knew things as easily as you know what color your shoes are? How amazing would that be? In this section we'll look at how you can use your claircognizance, or clear knowing.

In relationships it is critical to trust your vibes. In this day and age there are so many interactions made online rather than in person that you have no choice but to use your intuition to decide whether to work with or even go on a date with someone you don't know. Using your claircognizance to help sway you away or toward someone is one of the best ways to thin the herd. It can also keep you safe.

### *Try This!*
### Use Your Feelers to Get to Know People

Let's try an experiment. Use your claircognizant sense to tune in to a variety of people. To practice, you can use people you already know so you can get a handle on what it feels like. Think of five different people you know—make sure you mix it up with some you like and some you don't. The purpose here is to try and understand what your clear knowing feels like.

After you've selected your five, begin to think of them one at a time. Without restraining or judging, let yourself focus on the first three descriptors you get about them. For example, when I think of my husband, the first three adjectives I get for him are *protective*, *mushy*, and *fierce*. To me, it describes him to a T. When I think of a specific ex-employee, I immediately know that *immature*, *insecure*, and *untrustworthy* come to mind. By tuning in to people I am already familiar with, I can easily comprehend what the words feel like for me when I just know something about someone.

If you haven't already, go ahead and focus on your five people and experience, without questioning it, what three words you would use to describe them. These are things you just know. Recognizing how you have portrayed these people will help you moving forward in future relationships. Whether it's your personal or professional life, you can tune in to a person's energy to determine what you know about someone, even though you don't necessarily know them. By doing this, you can reduce any risk that's associated with that particular relationship. It can be your first meeting on a date, or it can be a decision about whether you want to get into business with someone new. Creating a rapport among new affiliations can increase your chances of getting ahead in life, and the more you trust your clear knowing, the more naturally it will begin showing you who people are. Trust it and it will decrease any risks connected to your new relationships.

## Addressing the Issue of Self-Sabotage

Everyone wants to be successful. But are we afraid to succeed? What actually comes with success? I mean, you put forth the effort, and you work very hard, doing whatever you can to get ahead. You might even set a goal and create a path to get there. But, somewhere along the way, something shifts. Just when you think you are going to succeed, you do something stupid.

Take my client Jan for instance. She had an important meeting, but she didn't have time to stop and get gas. She took so long getting ready because she was nervous thinking of what changes would happen in her life if she were to succeed. So, of course, she was driving along and *cough, cough, sputter*—the car died like a dinosaur during the Ice Age. There was no starting it because she was out of gas. She knew she needed it, but she didn't get it. Why did Jan take so long to get ready? Why the heck didn't she stop and take the five minutes to fill up the tank? Possibly because she didn't want to be late, but maybe it was because if she had made that meeting and she were to succeed, the benefits would have been too much for her to handle. And, maybe, she was self-sabotaging. Jan was scared to succeed.

Let's look at another example that may be a bit more practical and, yes, common. Your boss tells you they think you'd be perfect for a promotion that's just opened up in a different department, and you're all but guaranteed to get it. You've been comfortable where you are for a while, but this new position can line you up to becoming more successful overall. All you need to do is fill out the one-page application by end of business the next day and hand it in. You take the application, get excited, and think about it all day and night. The next day you just need to hand it in. But you don't do it. You don't hand it in. The promotion goes to someone else who wasn't as qualified but handed in their application. Why? Because you're lazy? Probably not. More likely because it made you nervous.

Is it so puzzling to figure out why we do this? There are a few reasons. If we don't try, it's not really like we sucked. Right? If we don't put the energy into succeeding, it's okay that we fail because we never really worked for it. Worse yet, if we succeed, what will that do to us?

I work with clients all the time who, after some serious soul searching and guidance, have finally figured out they are sabotaging themselves. It's taken them a long time to admit it because, after all, there is no one else to blame, and by admitting it, they now have to open themselves up to facing the reality that they have to make a decision. It's that pivotal moment in life when you can stay down or you can soar, possibly beyond your wildest imagination. This, my friends, can be scary.

Life is not all peaches and cream; it's not singing in the rain and splashing in the puddles with your rain boots on to protect you. Nope. It's exhilarating at times, absolutely, but it can also be scary to navigate through. Owning up to your shortcomings or even the skills you haven't quite acquired yet can be devastating. After all, it forces us to be honest with ourselves about our perceived limitations. Then what do you do? Well, that part is up to you. Own it so you can begin to change it.

You're never going to win if you don't try. You're never going to get ahead if you can't take that first step. You will, though it's clichéd, only regret the chances you don't take. From taking the shot to score in sports, to making the pitch to get the client, to asking the girl out, it's never going to happen if you don't take that chance. Sabotaging yourself by not even trying will always end in failure.

Instead of failing before you even start, how about attempting to succeed? Maybe, just maybe, if you stop self-sabotaging, you will start living your best life. Take it one step at a time. The second you realize you may be doing it, write down all the reasons you may be self-sabotaging—all the ways you might benefit if you stop denying yourself. Then try to make it happen! It may not be easy, but to move forward you have to start somewhere.

## Procrastination

As I sit here writing, I realize that one of my biggest deterrents to getting things done and finishing things up is procrastination. I also know, as I write this, that I can change my habits to increase my success. When we procrastinate, we stall our energy. Think of it like an arrow. We shoot the arrow out of a bow, so first we pick up the bow, the idea. Then, we load the arrow, putting together the plan. Next, we pull it back, cocking the arrow, or creating a strategy. Finally, we either release the arrow and let our energy soar, working to put the plan in action, or we drop the arrow because we waited too long. We procrastinated and stalled out our energy.

I don't know about you, but I am done stalling out. I want to move forward. I think you want to also, so let's do it together.

The first step is acknowledgment. I'll start. One thing I procrastinate with is calling people back. I get a number of calls a day, which I don't answer. Obviously, if it's a client or something important, I need to return their call, but I don't always check my voicemail right away. I wait, for a variety of reasons. Sometimes I'm in the middle of something. Sometimes I am not working that day. Sometimes I just don't feel like working right then in that moment. The problem, though, is if I wait too long, it makes me feel bad and it also makes the person wonder if I ignored them or at the very least why they didn't get a call back. (Sometimes I don't realize there is a voicemail. Those times don't count!) Worst-case scenario is someone who needed a session ASAP has now gone somewhere else, and I've lost their business. I am not only procrastinating, I am sabotaging my own business, and that is ridiculous!

Now it's your turn. What do you procrastinate about? Is it business/professional? Or personal? Is it holding you back from attaining what you want? Is putting off what you should be doing keeping you from moving ahead? Think about this because it's serious. Why are you doing it? Is it a theme in life? Are you afraid of something? Are you truly just lazy? Is it because you don't feel like dealing with the issue? Is there some other reason, like when my husband doesn't fix the drip in our rental property's shower because the person who put it in did it wrong and he will have to rip out half of the marble? Sometimes there is absolutely a legitimate reason. However, that doesn't give you a pass to procrastinate. I tell my husband to weigh the outcome. Procrastination long term in this circumstance can lead to a huge water bill or worse—replacing the entire shower. Fixing it may lead to replacing a portion of the marble. Which is worse? To me, for sure, it's the water bill and the possibility that the whole thing will need to be ripped out. Replacing or having to cut the marble is no big deal. So why procrastinate?

## Try This!
## Stop Procrastinating!

What will you do now? What would it take for you to stop procrastinating? Once you determine the reasons you are doing what you're doing, you can take it a step further and explore your possible outcomes using your intuition. If you continue to procrastinate, what will that do? Take a deep breath and tune in to your abilities. Then ask the following questions:

- What do I see happening?
- Will I lose a client?
  - A job?
  - An opportunity?
  - A position on a team?
  - A relationship?
  - Money?
- If I stop putting off what I need to do, what will the benefits be?
  - Can it increase my ability to do something?
  - Will it add to my wallet?
  - Will it make my life easier?
  - Will it add to my client base?
  - Will it open the possibility to gain a big account?

The list can go and on. You will never accomplish as much as you can if you stop putting things off. Now that you've tuned in and asked the hard questions, the next step is to figure out how to actually stop procrastinating. There is no magic pill to take, nor is there a button to press. Unfortunately, what's needed here is to continue tuning in to your intuition on a constant basis and weigh the two main questions above until you get to the balance you want.

Close your eyes. Using your clairvoyance and the rest of your gifts, visualize each benefit you'd reap if you stopped procrastinating, one at a time. As you do, move your eyes up and to the right (keeping your eyes closed). After you've done that, move your eyes back to center. Now, again, using your intuition, tune in to the next benefit and move your eyes up and to the right. Then, move them back to center. Do this with each and every advantage you'd have if you stopped procrastinating.

Next, do the same with each negative outcome that may happen if you continue putting things off, but when you focus on each one move your eyes down and to the left. Then, return your eyes to center. When you've completed your list of consequences from postponing your tasks, open your eyes.

Finally, imagine something that makes you really happy. As you do, with your eyes open, look up to the right and smile. Immediately, think of one of the benefits you'll have if you stopped procrastinating. Go through the list of happy thoughts and gains one by one. Then do the same with frustrating or negative thoughts and disadvantages while looking down and to the left.

When you are totally done, look up to the right and smile. You may or may not instantly stop procrastinating. It might take a few attempts, but every time you start to consider procrastinating instead of tackling something head on, repeat this exercise. Your mind's natural desire for happiness should begin to outweigh the desire to put things off!

Nobody said it would be easy. It takes work. It takes effort. You are trying to become the person you want to be, and that means taking strides toward change. Addressing your weak spots is the only way to take control of your destiny. If it is too scary to deal with them all at once, tackle them one at a time, but don't put it off. Procrastination keeps your focus consistently on the future, worrying or even agonizing about what you have to do. When you tackle the task, whatever it is, you will finish it and can live in the present moment without the concern over what may come. You can do it. Why wait?

There are so many chances to be taken in life. Without drawing on your intuition about which ones to take, the odds may very well be against you to succeed. When you become too afraid to go for it because the situation is scary and feels like too much of a gamble, you can lean on your gifts to help you try when appropriate. Those risks won't feel as insurmountable when you know you have an "in" with the universe. Even the big risks, like relocating, can be taken when you have that intuitive connection.

# CHAPTER 8
# Life and Location Changes

*Intuition takes into account the well-being of the whole:*
*the different agendas of our personal goals,*
*our company, the environment and the market,*
*and even the environment in which our market exists.*

—LAURA DAY, *PRACTICAL INTUITION FOR SUCCESS*

You've just read all about taking the chances, lessening the risks. Every so often, though, we need to intuit when to assume the risk and make the big changes. When you take a leap of faith in life, that opens you up to a different world, but it could possibly be a big mistake to actually jump in. To help sway toward success, leverage your intuition to find your true north. Your intuition can play a very important role in making big life changes like purchasing a house, relocating, and moving your place of business. Trusting your intuition to tell you when to go for it and when to walk away is equally important.

What motivates you? What changes do you need to make? When I do readings for people, I typically tune in to five basic things: relationship, money, career, family, and health, pretty much in that order. The emphasis is always on these topics but not because of me—it's what my clients want to know. These are our core concerns, at the center of our conscious thoughts. When you are feeling discomfort in some way in one of those areas, it can permeate throughout your psyche. Where do you go with questions about this stuff? You can tune in intuitively to your own gifts and figure out what the heck is going on and how to change to make it better.

Working with intuition affects every level of your being. Exercising your gifts in your personal life will help your career efforts and vice versa. It's never one or the other. Think of the basics. When you have a change in a relationship, use your intuitive GPS to figure out what direction to go. Notice I didn't say which type of relationship. Did you think personal? Business? Think of where your mind went. How did that feel? Do you feel like you are listening to your ESP regarding your relationships? Or should you tune in more?

Allowing your intuitive vibes to come through is part of the everyday battle we call life. Life can be a struggle, but riding the ups and downs is easier when you trust that you are doing the right things to make it better. Every area of your life is subject to changes—these can lead you toward good fortune or bring you into a hazard zone. You lessen the gamble that you're taking the right path when you use your sixth sense and connect to the energy of the universe, the ancient wisdom that's all around you. Not that every bad decision will lead you toward a pit of hellfire and brimstone, but those choices can definitely make life a little uncomfortable. Sometimes tuning in to less than positive energy can help you detect which way to lean.

Picking up on negative energy can absolutely serve a purpose. It can provide you with answers when you are trying to feel out a situation. It is helpful to use your clairsentience along with your other gifts when differentiating between good and bad, including investments. This came in handy when my client Alex came in.

"I have a million-dollar deal on the line," he said. "I need to know whether to buy this building so I can move my business into it and stop paying rent. But, before I purchase it, I have to make sure it's the right decision. I've checked in with my vibes, but I feel like it's a little too much for me to trust my own gifts right now—I need your backup."

Alex had come to me before, but it had always been concerning his personal life. This time obviously was different, and that put a bit more pressure on me to get it right. After all, buying a million-dollar building and moving your business into it is really a big deal. I didn't want to screw it up. I knew I had to come at it from all different angles to get the best possible information I could. I started by tuning in to my clairvoyance. I saw a beautiful, well-appointed office space, sitting empty. The emptiness made me wonder for a minute, but it was nice, so I ignored the vacancy.

"Well, so far, I see a beautiful building. I wonder why it's empty, but so far it looks good," I told Alex.

"I know, right? It seems like the perfect place. And it's so inexpensive!"

I asked the universe to help me out some more. I needed to understand if there was any reason not to buy it. Immediately, I could feel my clairsentience kicking in. I started tingling all over my body, which told me I was on to something. My clear feeling was definitely showing up. I began to feel a heaviness come over me. It started to feel like I was being sucked down into the earth, and the earth was filled with black, icky tar. I knew what was happening, and I knew why it was vacant and so inexpensive.

"Alex, I hate to break it to you, but I don't think you should do it. I feel a really bad energy there. It feels like the earth is reaching up to swallow whoever is there. And, even worse, it feels like the land and building are cancerous. I would be willing to bet there are some cancer patients that were either previous tenants or that are nearby. Check it out. And I'm sorry to break the bad news to you, but if you still feel strongly about it, do some research."

"Damn. That's what I was getting, but I wanted validation. I was hoping I was wrong!"

After getting the confirmation, Alex followed up and did his own investigation. It turns out the previous tenant that rented the building left and broke his lease because he was diagnosed with cancer. To add salt to the wound, Alex also discovered there were two other residents in the building next to it that were also diagnosed with cancer. He trusted in my clairsentient vibes and his own research and decided to stay where he was. It was not worth the risk.

Apparently, there had been a flower nursery next door that had been closed down years ago. Before it was closed, it used a ton of different chemicals that have since been banned. This feels like the reason for the problems in that area. My clairsentient vibes had tuned in to the energy of the earth where Alex's prospective building was, and I felt the negativity there, which I was able to share with him to provide a fuller picture of the property.

In this particular situation, Alex was having a hard time using his own intuition because he wanted the building so badly. He actually didn't want to trust his intuition, so he needed someone neutral to help him. Your own intuition should always be your first line of perception when it comes to making decisions. Checking in with your own vibes can give you the answers you need, but getting confirmation by tuning in a different way, with a different ability, or by gathering help from a professional coach or intuitive can help you further validate what you perceived.

## House Purchase

So often we feel our house. When we walk into a new space, we know right away if it feels right and should be ours. Our intuition, whether we recognize it as such or not, is working overtime when we are looking at new homes. Our imaginations take over when we've decided, in our minds, that it's our place. We start thinking about which bedroom will be for whom and whether our couch will fit in the living room. In other words, if we are feeling it, then we start to make it ours.

When you are vibing with a space, it is speaking to you. No matter if it is your next dream home or a soon-to-be place of business, the more it talks to you, the better. Everyone has their own preferences, which can be poles apart. That's why there are so many different styles of homes and offices. But, when one is right for you, you just know. Your hair stands up or you get butterflies in your stomach. It feels like you belong there. If you are checking out a new place, and it's something you've been hoping to do for a long time, even better. When the opportunity to invest finally arises it becomes hard to contain your excitement. Your heart gets excited. It's something you feel in your bones.

On the other hand, you need to be aware if you are feeling the opposite. Are your nerves twisting up? Does it feel like you might vomit? Are you breathing heavily? Sweating? Or maybe you have no reaction at all. Possibly, being in the space doesn't make you feel altered in any way—kind of like a void. Maybe you are feeling empty or hollow. Pay attention to your sixth sensory vibes if they are responding to a place with a feeling like you need to turn and run!

Jennifer always wanted to buy a house near Plymouth State College. She had always planned to purchase a rental house to lease out to college students. She'd thought about it and studied how much she could charge and for how many months. She also knew to plan ahead and make sure she worked into the rent the cost of having to repaint and repair everything that was ruined after the lease was up. After all, it was college students who would rent it out, and it was inevitable that there would be parties and a higher risk of damage. She was prepared and excited to do this.

When the opportunity arrived, she started looking in earnest. She had sold her residence and wanted to buy an investment house with the profits she had made. She started looking at all the houses for sale and working out the numbers and how much she'd have to charge based on the mortgages for the different houses. She was looking in the specific area she wanted, within one block from Plymouth State University, so she could have almost guaranteed rental income. She had it narrowed down to a couple of places. She had goosebumps just thinking of what she was about to do.

Then, at the last minute, she started feeling something was wrong. She was literally becoming nauseated just thinking about the situation. She told her realtor that she was backing out. She was done. She was not moving forward even though everything was lined up—she had the funds, she found a couple of great options, and they were located exactly where she wanted to be. But even with all of it seeming perfect, it was off. Jennifer broke out in a sweat until she finalized her decision to *not* go ahead with buying a house.

Even though no one quite understood what was happening, and why she'd changed her mind, she stuck to her guns and didn't budge. That was it. Her dream of owning a student rental near the college was over. She trusted her intuition, though at the time she had no reason to back it up. Until the announcement.

Shortly after all that went down, she discovered why she changed her mind. Plymouth State University announced that they were no longer letting students live off campus unless they were seniors. That cut at least half, probably more, of the rental market down. Houses, including all the ones Jennifer had just been interested in, instantly went up for sale. They couldn't unload them fast enough. People were left with mortgages they couldn't pay due to the lack of renters.

At the time, Jennifer had no idea why she was backing out. She knew, however, that there was no way she was going through with it. She had trusted her extrasensory perception to lead her in the right direction, thankfully. Although she was going against everything she'd ever wanted, she just knew there was no way she could go through with it.

Regardless of whether it was a personal or a professional investment, she would have lost her shirt. Paying attention to what her vibes were telling her, even though it went against what she had planned, saved her from losing everything she had made from the sale of her home. Although it was Jennifer doing this personally, she was doing it as a way to collect additional, mostly passive, income. If she had ignored her intuition, she would have been left in a bad situation. Thankfully, she was smart enough to listen to her intuition. Whether purchasing a building or moving into a rental, you can feel whether or not the place should be yours when you pay attention to what your vibes are telling you.

Your extrasensory perception can provide you with guidance for everything and anything. It also is a great source for solutions or alternative directions you might take to get your desired outcome. Every path to success will not be filled with fluffy, marshmallow-like clouds of sweet goodness—this we know. But it doesn't need to be lined with shards of glass waiting to mess you up. Usually, it's not quite this obvious. Heeding what your metaphysical senses are trying to impress upon you will definitely prove to be a much more enjoyable route. Although we know you are a success, suffering is not necessary to own that moniker. The absence of misery proves your strength in a more peaceful way.

## Relocating across the World

Buying a property or moving can be chaotic and exciting at the same time. Relocating in the same town is pretty simple. Moving to a new state can be a bit more hectic. Picking up your life and moving to a foreign country for work or personal reasons can activate all kinds of emotions. It might trigger fear or exhilaration and everything in between. When you do it because your intuition is telling you to, you have to be all in. You can't half-ass your intuitive directives if you are disrupting your entire life and possibly the lives of others.

When you are offered the opportunity to temporarily head up a new division in a foreign country so you can get it up and running and you could reap huge benefits, you agree. On the other hand, if you are thinking of doing it out of the blue and need some guidance about whether it will be a good move, checking in with your vibes will provide you with a great compass.

That is exactly what Helen did. A fabulous writer, she has an adventurous spirit. She has a dynamic energy that she freely shares with everyone around her. Her intuition had led her to voluntarily begin a new life in a new country. She shared her incredible story of intuitive guidance with me. In the summer of 1992, she was living in London, working as an international shipping journalist, traveling all over the world, and interviewing a huge range of people, from government ministers to dock workers. She had an interesting and varied group of friends, rented a room in a flat in Central London, and was, on the face of it, living a happy and successful life. It had always been her intention to make a living as a writer and to live in a dense urban environment, so those boxes were checked.

However, she shared with me that the city felt somehow closed to her, as if there was some secret, wonderful layer she couldn't penetrate and find, even though she participated fully in life there. She was always the last to leave any party and was often the one throwing the parties. She felt like she had too much energy for most people. She felt alone, like a coin rattling around in a tin box.

She went on vacation to New York to visit a friend who had moved there. So much about the city surprised her—its frenetic energy, the outspokenness of its people, the gloriously licentious attitude toward arts, sex, and fun! One incredibly hot, fetid night, she stood on Seventh Avenue and let herself be immersed in the teeming, relaxed, busy crowd flowing all around her. She suddenly knew she was home. Helen had never felt so much at home anywhere in her whole life. It was completely visceral and self-evident. She decided then and there that, no matter what, she had to come and live in this marvelous place.

It took her two years and many false hopes, including an interview at the *Wall Street Journal*. Eventually, she simply resigned from her job, feeling intuitively that if she made moving to New York the only possibility that could happen, it would happen. A few days later, she heard about an opportunity on a daily business paper in Manhattan. She applied and got the job. The paper sponsored her visa. She arrived just after dark on October 10, 1994. All she had was two suitcases and a job. That was it. No friends, nowhere to live. She had burned her life down to as close to a fresh start as she had ever done in her adult life.

When I asked Helen to describe how she felt in those scary and exhilarating first few months, she replied, "I was so happy I thought my hair might catch fire."

Within two years, she had become an associate editor covering the effects on the transportation industry of the newly burgeoning internet, had developed a wide and wildly interesting group of friends, lived in a lovely apartment in the endlessly funky East Village, and had met her future husband. It was scary, stepping off the cliff, and it might have seemed to many an act of lunacy to effectively throw away a whole life in London, but her intuition had told her, undoubtedly, it was the right thing to do. She trusted her gut instincts and changed her entire life.

I'm grateful to be able to say, as is she, that it all worked out very well indeed for Helen. Not only do I get to be her friend now, but she has found her true north, the place she belongs, along with the people she deserves and who are beyond lucky to be part of her extended circle.

## Using Your Intuitive Compass

Where's your true north? Where do you fit in? Or where can you step out of your comfort zone to discover who you want to be rather than who you are? Do you ever stop to simply check in with your metaphysical compass? The intuitive energy we pick up on can direct us to our true north, or where we feel guided or drawn to, like a magnetic compass.

### *Try This!*
### Finding Your True North

Let's figure out where your true north is, where you would prosper should you make a geographical change in your living space or your workplace. Stand up in the middle of the room or wherever you are, making sure there is nothing within four to five feet of you. Slowly turn around with your eyes closed three times. The point of this is you don't want to know which direction you are facing. Keep your eyes closed. Settle yourself so you don't feel dizzy. Then begin, slowly, to move your body in a circle again. If you feel energetically pulled toward a specific direction, take a step that way. Then stop and turn again, still in a relaxed manner. Take a step toward whichever way you feel pulled. One more time, turn unhurried in a circle. Stop, breathe, and then take a step when you feel drawn one way or the other. Finally, check in with your energy, and take two steps in the direction you feel attracted to and keep your body facing that way. Then, open your eyes.

Where are you in relation to where you began? Which direction are you facing? Is it the same as where you started out? Or totally different? Think about what is located in the direction you are facing. Is there a house or a building you'd like to check out? Is there a specific town? Obviously, you don't have an exact measurement as to the location you are facing, but you can generalize it. How does it feel energetically? Does it feel right? Wrong? Does it resonate with you at all? Or do you have absolutely no connection yet to where you are facing? Do you know what the opportunities may be?

Take it to the next level and look at a map—there are multiple apps and websites available. See what might be within ten miles from you, headed the way you were facing. Do you recognize any possibilities? Does it make you feel excited? How about if you go twenty miles out or to the next town? Or even three towns over? If you are so compelled, you can even go all the way to other countries. This is about your true north. You may have found you are exactly where you need to be and that is okay too. There is no wrong answer, but there could be a right answer. It may actually spur you on to make some much-needed changes. Your energy is pulling you toward where you need to be or what you need to do next. It might be a great idea to make some lifestyle changes in order to become the best you you can be. Use your intuitive GPS to jump-start yourself in the right direction!

Intuition is an incredibly strong and dynamic tool. It can help you with most of your major life changes—whether to make the transformation or not. These types of life-altering choices should not be made lightly. Deciding to make a significant purchase or an international move is fraught with uncertainty. Using all the tools you have at hand can increase your chances of success. Be open to receiving and perceiving the intuitive messages however they come through, remembering that your guides will use every way they can to facilitate your awareness.

# CHAPTER 9

# Other Ways to Tune in to Your Intuition

*Synchronicities happen when we listen to the soft voices.*
*They are life's little way of reminding us to pay attention,*
*to follow the signs, and to watch the path in front of us as it unfolds.*

—LYN RAGAN, *SIGNS FROM THE AFTERLIFE*

Sometimes your intuition speaks to you in different ways. Remember, the easier it is to understand your intuitive vibes the better. We are multifaceted people. Therefore, we need a variety of ways to tap into our metaphysical senses. Obviously, we have all the clairs, but we need to receive those messages in order to process them. I like to think of it like the electrical companies. There are two different charges on our bill: the first is the fee for the actual electrical energy we use, and the second is the fee for the supplier charge. While our intuition costs us nothing to use, it can be broken up in the same way—the actual intuitive information we receive and how it is provided to us.

We can consider ourselves extremely fortunate that we have a plethora of methods to access our intuitive guidance. The clairs are generally intangibles; we can't physically see them or hold them. Our tools, depending upon what we are using, can be both intangible and tangible. And then, there are synchronicities and signs, both of which we recognize with our physical senses.

These are external events or situations sent by the universe, our guides, and deceased loved ones to answer our questions and provide us with direction and, sometimes, just to let us know we are not alone.

## Synchronicities

When you begin noticing coincidences and things that shouldn't go together but do, those just may be synchronicities. Analytical psychologist Carl Jung used the word *synchronicity* in his writings to describe meaningful coincidences that seemingly have no causal connection or relationship. These synchronicities show up to assist us in recognizing our intuition, and in fact they give us insight that we may not have otherwise had.

Synchronicities are a pretty common occurrence, although we don't always recognize them as such. It usually takes a few or even more synchronistic events to happen before we begin putting them together. Frequently, these coincidences happen daily—some are stronger than others. Unless they are obvious, we may never notice them.

For instance, if you are thinking of someone out of the blue and run into them shortly after, that is your intuition essentially showing you a flash of what's to come. When I do readings for people, quite regularly I will get a flash of one of my other clients beforehand. As often as this happens, it makes me pause. Later that day or maybe the next I get a call or an email that they want to set up another appointment. It doesn't matter if I haven't talked to them in a month or five years, it always works the same way. It is inevitable that I will hear from them, and soon.

Let's pretend you are looking for a job. You are trying to decide whether to look for your full-time forever job or just something temporary until you figure out what it is for sure that you want to do. You've narrowed it down to getting a job in an office where you can utilize the skills you just graduated with or a temporary server position at a restaurant where you can make some great tips. You keep thinking about it but don't mention your dilemma later on while you are hanging out with friends.

Out of nowhere, your friend says, "I had the best lunch today at Texas Roadhouse. I walked in and there was a HELP WANTED sign. That would be a perfect place to make some good tips if I didn't already have a job!"

Imagine your jaw is now on the floor because you hadn't mentioned looking for a waiting job anywhere. And then, your other friend chimes in.

"I wish I had waited and done that first. I regret that I jumped in and started full time already. I should have done waitressing or something first."

There are your synchronistic events. Two seemingly unconnected answers to your question: first, where you might be able to find a serving job, and second, whether you should do that or work in your office career first. *Bam!* Pay attention! The universe is trying to tell you something, and it is not convincing you using your straight-up ESP, so it is proving it with using a more in-your-face method. There is really no denying that.

## Signs

You've been introduced to symbolism, which essentially is internal signs. Symbols are often the way we are able to perceive our intuitive guidance. Our guides, the universe, and even our deceased loved ones will use any method they possibly can to get you information and frequently symbols are the easiest and quickest method. Essentially, these visual stimuli are a way to receive information, and it's about time you are introduced to the more palpable form, signs. Signs are the things that show up, externally, to emphasize or validate your intuition. Our intuition uses a mix of methods to get through to us—signs are one of the few tangibles that help us recognize our intuitive hits. Having something tangible gives us evidence we can hold or physically see. That proof helps validate our intuition.

Signs are often noticed through synchronicities. Simply explained, this means that you'll notice something externally that answers a question or seems to be a direct response to something you have been thinking about. When we are trying to process information, we may ask for a sign to validate what we intuitively or even literally believe to be the solution or answer. For example, if you are debating whether to go back to school as you are zoning out watching television and suddenly a commercial comes on for a college, that can be a sign that, yes, it may be a good time to put your scholarly hat back on. If you change the channel and an ad is playing about a textbook rental site, then bingo. The universe is trying to let you know, for sure, to get your butt back to school!

Signs come in so many forms and are very common ways for our deceased loved ones to let us know they are around. This just came up today in a reading I did with Betty Sue. We were wrapping up the session, during which her sister who had just passed had come through and acknowledged a bunch of things in Betty Sue's life. All of a sudden, I saw an image of a red bird. I asked her if a bird meant anything to her. In the moment, she said no, she had no idea, but right as we were getting ready to hang up, she realized what it was:

"A couple of days ago, I had been thinking of my sister all morning, wishing she was with me or that she could send me a sign. A few minutes later, I noticed two birds on the ground, cardinals. Then one flew away. The other was just staring at me. I was nervous because there was a cat watching it. I walked over to it, expecting it to fly away, but it didn't move. So I got right up next to it and it still didn't move. It didn't look hurt, it just watched me. I gently picked it up and put it up higher on a hanging planter because I was worried that cat would get it if it stayed on the ground. Still, it didn't move or get stressed or try and fly away. It just kept watching me. I went inside to get bird seed. When I went back out to check on her and feed her, she was gone."

I confirmed for her what she already knew. The bird was a sign from her sister, Carolyn. She was letting her know she heard her and that she'd always be there for her. It was a pretty clear sign and one that, although it took her a minute to remember, was pretty evident. Signs can and will show up to help you identify that your loved ones are around to answer questions you may have or even to guide you in the direction you may need to go.

So how can you use signs to your advantage for work? Easy. Ask the question. Wait for a sign. Can't get any easier, right? However, you must be present and pay attention to what shows up. It can slip right past you, otherwise. Let's say you do custom auto fabrications. You want to know whether to put money into sales and marketing or hire a new technician. Ask the universe which direction would be best for you. Sometimes you only need one sign to get the message. Other times you may wait for additional signs to verify the first one was truly a sign.

Then, let's say you are headed down the highway, on your way home, and you notice a billboard you've never seen before. It is blank, but it says, YOUR BUSINESS BELONGS ON HERE! TO INCREASE YOUR SALES, ADVERTISE! Now you have a choice. You can ignore the huge freaking sign you just saw, or you can be smart and understand the universe is helping you any way it possibly can to steer you in the right direction. The only downside to this incredible sign is that others will see it too—so pay attention! Don't wait too long to make your decision and go for it!

## Combining Synchronicities, Signs, and Intuitive Guidance

Synchronistic events and signs don't always show up when we expect them. Rather, they rarely come when we want them to—they appear when you are ready to perceive them. You might ask the universe to validate something and it might not show up for a while. However, you might not realize that circumstances can come full circle to show you that what you are doing is exactly what you are supposed to. In other words, you receive signs along the way, but you might not get total corroboration that you've done the right thing until you actually do it!

This is why it is so crucial to trust in all the different modes of intuitive awareness. If you are trying to figure out something at work, you have a multitude of options to use to get some metaphysical answers.

Dr. Tammy Nelson, an international sex therapist, author, and presenter, shared one of her many life-changing stories of intuition with me. She was trying to think of a way she could make some income without doing just individual counseling. Otherwise, she knew she needed more hours in the day! She was already stretched way too thin. She got it in her head that she would try to figure out some options during her weeklong stay at a yearly conference called the Networker Symposium in Washington, DC. This is a training conference run and organized by the Psychotherapy Networker, which is a full-service facilitator for training programs and a monthly self-titled magazine. Tammy was there not only to participate in the workshops, but also to lead and teach her own pre-conference workshop about sex therapy.

While there, she was approached by many people, all suggesting she teach her own workshop class in Washington, DC, because there was virtually no sex therapy training available in the area at all. However, Tammy lived in Connecticut. She did not feel drawn to DC at all. As a matter of fact, she felt more of an aversion to the area because of the political climate. She was also already super busy and really didn't have the time, but people continued to insist she would be really well received and she should try it.

"Just come on down and do it! They will love you here!" was what they asserted.

So she made her decision. If she could get space—without spending a ton of money on travel, setup, and the venue—and if the whole situation easily fell into place, she would do it.

While she was thinking about it, she got a phone call from a friend she had taken the class with. She told him of what she was contemplating. She didn't say much else.

He asked her, "Do you have a place to hold it?"

"No. I don't think I'll find a place where it will be financially feasible, so it probably won't happen," she confessed.

"Oh, well I know of a great school where they rent out teaching rooms and conference rooms pretty inexpensively. You should contact them." He gave her all the information.

Tammy called the school and realized this could actually be a possibility. The initial contact at the Networker Symposium had apparently already gotten back to the school, so by the time Tammy reached out to them, they knew exactly who she was and shared they would offer her a discounted rate as a professional courtesy. Now it felt like she couldn't turn it down.

She made it happen. She created a two-day workshop, and people signed up and came to it. In fact, people loved it. It was a total success. Not only did she create something new, she paid attention to the synchronistic chain of events that got her here. She decided to do it some more.

Six years later, she has created a whole institute in Washington, DC, with many classes and offers certification programs. She is not even altogether sure how it happened. She kept getting intuitively drawn down there. It continued to grow and get a lot more complicated. And, besides that, she became bicoastal, living in California for two weeks and Connecticut for the next two. Just when she thought she might close the institute down, she was intuitively led to create a new certification for sex and couples therapy. She has people coming from all over the world to get certified by her and her institute. She made it a hybrid program, part online and part at the institute, knowing it would not be convenient for her to continue traveling to DC or for others to travel consistently from their homes as well.

Then, because she listened to her intuition and the synchronistic events that kept popping up, she received an offer from an accredited Los Angeles school. They were creating a new PhD program in sex therapy and wanted Tammy to help. Of course they did—after all, now she was in Los Angeles as well. She wondered how she would be able to do that and still get students for her own school. Putting it out to the universe, she thought again if she was shown a way to make it work, she would do it. She got an email shortly after: "We will take all your students, and we will tell all our students they have to come to you to get their certification." How could she turn it down now? The universe for sure was conspiring in her favor.

Then, because she is so good at this, obviously, she asked the universe for a sign. She wanted to know what to do next to increase her passive income. That afternoon, she got her mail and there was a *Psychotherapy Networker* magazine. She thought to herself, "That's a sign," and waited, trusting her intuition and the universe, though she had no idea what would happen next.

The call came later that day. The Networker asked Tammy to tape an eighteen-hour online program, pretty much a one-and-done event, that they would offer. In return, they offered to feed everyone directly back to Tammy's institute program for classes and certifications before they could take the next step with them.

Tammy listened to her intuition. She paid attention to the synchronicities that kept popping up. She recognized the signs. And, most importantly, she listened. She has created many new outlets for herself, created training pro-grams, and created many new passive income revenue streams.

Tammy's story is a perfect example of how the universe can provide you with answers, often in ways that you aren't expecting. The responses may not come as soon as you want, but be patient—you will get them in time. Also, let this be a wake-up call to be observant. Participate in your life by staying on alert for your guidance to show up.

## Utilize Your Intuition, However It Comes

Trusting your instincts can come in handy when you are looking for guid-ance. You've got options—there are so many different ways to tune in to your natural gifts. The easier, the better, though, right? So why not take advantage of every method possible!

It's interesting. So frequently, just when we think we aren't using our intu-ition, we realize we've been using it all along. Whether it is a gut feeling we are getting or a synchronistic flash, it's not always critical to recognize it as intuition—as long as we follow it. One of the reasons we don't need to worry that we aren't aware we are using it is because when we don't go against our vibes, it keeps everything, including our energy, calm. It is when we start swimming against the current that it becomes more apparent we are not fol-lowing our personal GPS. Things are easier when we are not trying to fight the natural flow.

The more familiar we are with distinguishing signs and synchronicities and everything else that goes along with it, the more apt we are to identify our intuitive messages more often. It won't stop; rather, it increases with awareness, as does your ability to thrive and become the best you you can be.

# CHAPTER 10

# Shape a Better You

*It's never too late and you're never too old*
*to live your dreams and find success!*

—VIC JOHNSON, *IT'S NEVER TOO LATE AND YOU'RE NEVER TOO OLD*

There are infinite possibilities to shape your life when you make the most of everything life has to offer. In both business and your personal life, there are facets of your life that can be adjusted. Similar to getting tune-ups for your car, performing maintenance checks periodically keeps you on track. There are endless updates available that you can use to guide you on your life path and keep you going in the direction that feels right. Specifically, when you take a look at all that you are and all that you want to be, it becomes increasingly obvious that there is always room for improvement.

## Using Intuition to Better Yourself

We go to the gym. We diet. We go to school. We work hard. We do everything to better ourselves, so why not use our intuition to help us make changes? It is silly to not utilize every tool in our toolbox. Let's think about this for a minute. How would you like to better yourself? What do you think would make you a better version of you? When we renew ourselves and we go deep, we find what matters. Grab your gear and get ready, because now that you know how to use your intuition, it's the perfect time to look back at who you were and think forward to who you will become.

Have you ever wondered what kind of life you'd have if you'd made choices other than the ones you did? Not only do you have an opportunity to choose which direction you want to go now, but you have your intuition to check in with to see how your options would work out. One of the best things you can do to better yourself is to check in with your vibes. I had a client who did just that.

Alicia came to see me for a reading. She wasn't sure why, but she'd made an appointment and was sitting in my office. After going over a lot of what I was picking up, I started feeling something else.

"Are you thinking of making a big change?" I asked her.

Alicia responded by presenting me with a confused look. Then she laughed and said, "No?"

"No, really! I am picking up that you are about to embark on a life-changing mission," I continued.

"Not that I know of."

"Okay, well, give me a minute here."

I tuned in to her energy some more. I was getting that she was gearing up to make some major changes. Then I started feeling that she knew what it was, but she hadn't committed to it yet. It was almost as though she had an opportunity sitting up on a shelf, like a much-wanted toy, just waiting to be taken down and played with.

"Listen, Alicia. I feel like you are already thinking of a potential life-course adjustment."

"Hmmm. I still don't know what you mean," she responded.

"For something this big, you would know what I'm tuning in to. Are you sure?"

"Yup. No idea."

I took another breath and tapped into the ether.

"All right, I think I get it now. Are you going back to school? Are you totally changing careers? Or creating a new career?"

"Oh my God! I have been wanting to do this so badly! I have been try-ing to tune in to my intuition to see if it is something I can do!" Alicia was excited now.

"I see you going to school. I feel like you are going to start nursing school. I also feel like this is a total change for you because I see you in business right now. Does this make any sense?"

"Wow! Yes!" she agreed. "That makes total sense! But I haven't done any of it yet," she said, a bit sad.

"Don't worry, you will," I told her with absolute certainty.

"I have to tell you—I have been thinking about this for about six months but I don't know how it will be possible. I am too old! I haven't made any moves yet."

"I am feeling like you kind of intuited this for yourself, which is interest-ing because you are telling me you don't think it's possible. And, girl, you are definitely not too old," I responded as it came to me that this was her idea.

"Well, let me explain."

Alicia went on to tell me how she was at her office job one day a while back, and suddenly, she had a flash of herself sitting at the desk. It was like she was looking down at herself. She said that was strange enough, but when she questioned what she had seen, she heard, "Wait."

"Did you understand what you were seeing?" I asked her.

"No, not until I went home later."

When she got home from work, exhausted, she started dinner for herself, her husband, and her daughter. Then she told them she needed to have a few minutes to herself to meditate, and they said they would finish cooking. That, she said, was unusual, but she figured they knew she was tired. She went into her bedroom and sat down on her bed. She took a few deep breaths and then asked the universe to show her what she was supposed to know. She knew there was more because she had heard "Wait." So she waited. And then waited some more.

She meditated for about five minutes before the answers came. She felt goosebumps and then saw herself in a hospital room. She was not, how-ever, the patient. She was standing up. She was wearing a uniform and had a stethoscope wrapped around her neck. And, she just knew, intuitively, that she was a nurse. She could feel it in her bones.

She remained on her bed for a few more minutes, but the goosebumps went away and she saw no more. She had no idea what it meant, and she went downstairs to have dinner. The funny thing was, she didn't think of it for the rest of the night. But, when she woke up the next morning, it was all she could think of. She was confused, though. She had a great job, though she didn't feel fulfilled. The thought of her as a nurse made her tingle. But she didn't know how she'd be able to go back to school to get her nursing degree, so she ignored what her intuition was telling her—that is, until she came to see me.

"I feel like an incredible opportunity is on its way soon, so be open to it," I told her. "And make sure you let me know when it shows up!"

A month later, Alicia messaged me. She was driving and she saw a bill-board advertising an online college where she could get her nursing degree in less than two years, since she already had a bachelor's in business. It reso-nated with her deeply. She trusted her intuition, applied, and got in. She was going to be a nurse! She was so ready to better herself. Already, she said, she felt lighter and happier. I was so excited for her and told her I couldn't wait for her to start working on her dreams!

Alicia's story is a perfect example of listening to your intuition to better yourself and build a better, more fulfilling life. Luckily, Alicia listened to what her senses were telling her and followed through on what she knew was a fundamental step toward being an improved version of herself. Remember, when we are conscious and aware of our intuition, we get to be who we want to be. And that can be anyone.

### Try This!
### Who Are You, Really?

Who do you want to be? How can you better yourself and become your authentic self? By living your life on purpose. Think about who you are right now, in this moment. Who would you be if you weren't you? Your answers to the following questions can help you figure this out! Write down your answers!

- Who would you be if you weren't you?

- What do you want people to think about who you are?

- What is be your ideal career?

- Where would your ideal home be?

- What are your top three things to do?

- What is the ideal image of yourself?
  - Looks
  - Personality
  - Finances

- Are you happy?

Now that you've asked your conscious mind these questions, it's time to review your answers. What did you think of your answers? Did any of them surprise you? Did they feel familiar? When you review everything you've written, does it seem like there is a common theme? Do you feel like you're too old to change? Too young to begin?

Okay, it's time to make some intuitive adjustments. How do you get from where you are now to where you want to be? Most people, once they are established in life, have a very difficult time trying to change. They have a family or a career, and to mix all of that up could create chaos—for everyone. But what if it were a better life for everyone after the chaos? Would you make the changes? Would you release the fear and concern that may be holding you back? Come on, let's do this together!

You've asked the tough questions and hopefully have gotten honest insight into the type of person you want to be. It's time to visualize that happening and imagine who that person would be. Obviously, you can't change your height, but mostly everything else can be updated to reflect the best you. Get comfortable, this is going to take some work. Close your eyes. Use your meditative breathing techniques to relax yourself until you feel ready. Here we go.

Visualize yourself, your current self, standing in a black room; there's no other color but you. Look at what you are wearing, how your hair looks, what's on your feet. Behind you in that room there is a television—a large one hanging on the wall. Right now, it's still off, so there's no imagery on the screen. Imagine the screen is beginning to turn on, slowly, and as it does, you can see yourself as you imagine yourself to be if you could be a better version of you. Notice what your body looks like. Pay attention to whether it's different than it is now. What clothes are you wearing, if any? What does your hair look like? Really see this image of yourself. Do you recognize that person looking back at you? Take a minute to let it soak in.

When you are ready to move on, you see another TV to the right of the first one, kind of floating. The screen is black. As the light coming from the initial television begins to dim a bit, still showing you the image of yourself, this new TV begins slowly lighting up. As it does, you can see a location on the screen. You see your ideal home, in your desired landscape. You can tell what part of the country or the world you are in based on the type of home and what the background scenery shows you. If you look closely, in front of the door, you can see this new version of yourself that you viewed in the first television. You have a big smile on your face, standing there in your new, best possible environment for you. Enjoy that setting for a minute. Do you see anyone else there with you? Significant other, children, and so on. Stay there for another moment. Soak in the home, where it is, and who is with you. Then, take a deep breath.

To the right, another screen begins lighting up as the last one fades a bit. This one may be a bit more in depth, so just let it happen. As the imagery comes into focus, you see yourself in your career. Notice what it is. Pay attention to where you are. See what state or country you're in and the environment. What are you doing? Really see it. Are you helping someone? Are you on stage? Are you writing? Are you inside or outside? Are you wearing a uniform? A suit? Comfortable clothes? Really visualize on that screen what you are doing. Are you sitting at a desk, planting flowers, speaking to a crowd of people, teaching children? Whatever it is, see it with clarity. Keep watching the screen as it continues to show you in your element, working in a career that is perfect for you. As you continue to watch, you see this version yourself turn and look at you with a big smile. You are in the perfect career. Enjoy this video of yourself for a little while longer.

When you've visualized all the details of your perfect career, turn to the right a bit, to the next television screen. As the previous TV fades slightly, this one begins to light up, slowly bringing images into focus. As you watch, you can see your finances playing out on the screen. On a table in front of you, there is money. Do you see just a few coins? Stacks of hundred-dollar bills? Something in between? As you watch the screen, notice if you see more money falling onto the table or if you notice it falling out of the vision or both. Do you see yourself there, holding the money? Or throwing it away? This is your best possible financial situation playing out on the screen. If you don't see enough on the table, imagine there is a huge funnel above the table that you can see on the TV. As you look at the funnel, you begin to see money floating down through it on to the table, creating an overflow of cash available to you. Keep seeing this on the television screen. Enjoy the cashflow you see, knowing this is out there for you, when you are in the perfect career, in the perfect place. Continue watching this video for a bit, until it feels real and comfortable to you.

Now focus on the final television screen. As it begins to light up, the previous one fades a little. This one is interesting. You are in the middle of the screen, laughing and smiling! You are so happy! This is your ideal life, the best version of you possible. Notice if there is anyone there with you. Also, see where you are. Are you back at the original home? Are you at work? Are you somewhere else? Pay close attention to the expressions on any faces that are there besides yours. Are they happy as well? Sad? Angry? Ecstatic? Look back to yourself on the screen. Are you still laughing and smiling and enjoying everything there is to enjoy? Make sure you are! Watch yourself enjoying life for a few minutes. Let it really sink in.

Now, when you are ready, look back at all the screens. As you do, they begin fully lighting up. See your ideal life opening up to you, in full color, bright, happy, and contented. Watch all the images on each television until they all begin to merge into one giant movie screen. Enjoy the show!

Now, look at yourself standing in that room. You may see flashes of your current life floating in, but that's okay. You might notice your clothing has changed and you are wearing what you had on in the movie you just watched of your best life. You might notice your body has changed a bit and your hair too. You may also see cash overflowing from your pockets. Fantastic! Take a deep breath and open your eyes to your old reality.

You are now ready to live your best life! You've tuned in to your intuition and visualized everything you want. The last step is making it happen. If you've imagined a different career, start tuning in to your intuition to determine how you can make that happen. Does it involve training or going back to school? If so, start researching how you can do that. If being the best you involves moving, how can you make that happen? Again, research it. Look into homes and prices where you want to be. If you have other people in your life and family, how can you all work together to help you become the best you? Start the conversation while you do your research. Every day is a second chance.

The bottom line is this: to become a better version of you, you must put in some work. You can't just sit on your hands and expect everything to change. It's not about sacrificing what and who you are; it's about becoming who you want to be, who you need to be.

In order to leverage your intuition for your career, you need to follow through with your visions and commit to making the changes. You never know—opening your senses can be the catalyst you need to begin leading others. You just may discover your values are driving you to the next stage in your life. Don't worry—you've got this!

# CHAPTER 11

# Leading with Intuition

*Facts and intuition are false opposites.*
*Leaders should listen to their intuition and instincts*
*and allow others to do the same because they are subconscious,*
*fast ways of processing, aggregating and then accessing*
*evidence to reach a swift conclusion. Trust your gut.*

—PHIL DOURADO, *THE 60 SECOND LEADER*

Let's face it—not everyone is cut out to be a leader. Not everyone wants to be a leader. However, there are so many who are born to lead and are natural leaders. Whether you are leading a team at work, are a coach, or run things at home, you can become a better leader by using your intuition.

You don't really need to rely on your intuition to know that you'll get more from someone when they are comfortable with you or when they feel good about the situation they are in. Whether it's a team you are leading or clients you are wooing, it's common knowledge that you catch more flies with honey. Obviously, we are not flies, but we do react better when we are relaxed, so we can use our intuition to determine what will make our customers or clients happy.

# Become a Better Leader

Back in the caveman days, intuition was a critical part of life. Humans needed to constantly be connected to their intuition to stay safe. They were only trusted to lead a group if they were strong. Being strong wasn't just a physical thing. It also meant they were able to find food and provide shelter without getting everyone killed in the process. Cavemen couldn't mess around.

Luckily, being a leader now isn't usually a life-or-death situation, but you still have people depending on you. How can you be that person that people want to follow? You not only need to be good at what you do; you also have to give your team or your company someone to believe in. You have to be the kind of leader you'd want. Who would that be?

Great leaders inspire everyone to follow and take action. More than that, they create a culture in which people feel free to act. Herminia Ibarra knows leadership. She is the Cora Chaired Professor of Leadership and Learning at INSEAD, the founding director of the leadership transition executive education program at INSEAD, and an author who writes about business and leadership. She writes, "When we act like a leader by proposing new ideas, making contributions outside our area of expertise, or connecting people and resources to a worthwhile goal (to cite just a few examples), people see us behaving as leaders and confirm as much."[9]

These good leaders encourage their subordinates to think for themselves and welcome the offering of ideas and thoughts. Self-absorption is not a characteristic that should ever be used to describe a skilled leader. The best leaders motivate their team to want to succeed. Being a great leader doesn't just happen; it comes from within and is developed further by your actions. The best leaders can bring value to the table through ideas, concepts, and contributing as much as, if not more than, those they are leading.

The first rule of leadership is knowing that investing in your people, team, group, and so on will cause your business to grow exponentially. This, simply put, means putting time and energy into your group. You need to gain

---

9. Herminia Ibarra, *Act Like a Leader, Think Like a Leader* (Boston, MA: Harvard Business Review Press, 2015), 4.

the respect of your team in order to get what you need out of them. No one will respect you unless you respect them. They may be afraid of you, or fear for their job, but they will not hold you in high esteem if they can't trust that you have their backs.

In order to become a better leader, you should look to a combination of intuition and reason, sometimes known as your inner and outer worlds. You need to figure out what will stimulate your team to build a successful business. In order to do that, you can utilize all your talents—both physical, worldly skills (outer) and metaphysical (inner) skills. Before you decide how, you need to determine what the end goal is. It doesn't have to be the final outcome, but you must have goals along the way that others can aspire to reach. Leaders who are able to access both sides of their brain in a cooperative way will invariably be better naturally at managing groups because they use everything they've got.

Way back when I was the controller of a company, I helped set up a day of aptitude and personality training for all the department heads. We went off campus to an establishment that specialized in making companies better by matching their employees to the jobs they were best suited for. This applied to the leaders as well.

They got us all set up and administered the Myers-Briggs test. When we finished, we plotted our answers on a chart and connected the dots. Most people were mostly on the right or the left sides and mostly on top or below the center line. My chart was a perfect diamond. The test facilitator explains that I was perfectly right and left brain balanced, logical as well as intuitive, extroverted and introverted all at the same time. This, they said, was a compassionate leader in the making. It made perfect sense to me, and the balance seemed to match with my value system.

Developing core values that your team can relate to is important anytime you are in a managerial position. Bringing your team in to create the value system with you will create bonding within the team. Tapping into your intuition will help to create that list of values. The following is a compilation of possible values. Go through them and check which ones fit with your style and your leadership.

- Authenticity
- Balance
- Compassion
- Creativity
- Dedication
- Fairness
- Family
- Friendship
- Fun
- Growth
- Happiness
- Hard work
- Honesty
- Integrity
- Intuition
- Justice
- Learning
- Recognition
- Respect
- Spirit
- Stability
- Truth

When you share the same values with your group, they will feel more comfortable and will have more respect for your authority and your leadership role. It will help them connect with you and work harder for you and will make the team stronger.

Now that you've bonded with your group, figure out what your vision for the team is. Maybe you already have a real one or maybe not. First, you must decide what kind of leader you are. Do you utilize your inner or outer world to get information you need? Do you use both? Below is a checklist.

Mark whether you would use your intuition or your external senses in order to handle the situations.

| Intuition | Situation | External |
|---|---|---|
| | Try to acquire a new client | |
| | Make a decision | |
| | Learn about the people I work with | |
| | Figure out my next steps | |
| | Determine which team members fit with which clients | |
| | Design a website | |
| | Create / develop a marketing plan for a client | |
| | Create / develop a marketing plan for my own business | |
| | Design a logo | |
| | Solve problems with staff | |
| | Determine who needs a promotion | |
| | Deal with computer issues | |
| | Determine what someone wants | |
| | Understand what drives someone | |
| | Predict outcomes in situations | |

Hopefully, you've discovered a little bit about how you process situations as a leader. Using your intuition as well as your external senses gives you a definite advantage. Did you find you favored one over the other? Are you more inner world? Or more outer world? Most people will find they use a blend. If you're like me, you'll discover you are more intuitive, and you will trust your instincts more than analytical data.

Take for instance understanding what drives a person. If you are tuning in and trying to feel their energy or you use your clairvoyance to see what they enjoy doing, you are using your intuition. If, alternatively, you do research to find out what that same person is into, you may be leaning more toward your external senses. If you do a little of both, you might use a more balanced approach to discover what drives a person. Figuring out the methods you use can point you toward what you might be able to enhance a bit more to become a great leader.

## Using Vision to Lead

Using your intuitive gifts opens a new and improved level of awareness when you are in charge. It gives you options not otherwise utilized. American scholar Warren Bennis wrote, "Leadership is the capacity to translate vision into reality."[10] The situations in the earlier table are generic in that you can apply them to most leadership roles. You can tune in to your vibes to see how you would handle each. Think of your intuition as a secret weapon and use it to be a better leader.

Choosing to not go it alone and instead bring your entire team into the intuitive process is a sign of a true leader. Listen, they don't all have to buy into your way of doing things, but they can contribute in their way, to start. Once you get them on board, working together, they may begin to experience their own intuitive hits, those aha moments of clarity. They may have no idea where the ideas came from, but they showed up and they were good!

When you work in a group, your intuition becomes heightened. This is where the really juicy, good stuff comes in. Imagine sitting in a circle, kicking ideas around. You've probably done this before in some capacity—in a formal or more relaxed format. You start feeding off each other and the energy just starts to flow through the group, one suggestion building from the one before. This tends to happen when people tune in in any type of creative or intuitive way. It's the way our minds work.

As leaders, we can create an intuitive group, a think tank if you will, to collectively tune in to the questions leaders need to answer. Pretend you are leading a team that has been tasked to sell a new, healthy energy drink. Not only do you have to decide on flavors, but you have to put together packaging and sell it to the client before you will get the deal.

The good thing about this is you have your entire team to work with, so collect your team and put the first question to them: What is the first flavor

---

10. Warren Bennis, *On Becoming a Leader: The Leadership Classic* (Philadelphia, PA: Basic Books, 2009), 188.

we should offer? This can be logically determined by market research. We know, as good leaders, that we should use a mix of traditional data and intuition, so we won't throw away the opportunity to employ every asset we have to our benefit. But what we absolutely can do to make it better than plain "raspberry" is use our combined intuitive minds to come up with a more exciting name. Ask them to focus on what they hear people calling this new drink in their mind, using their clairaudience. When we make a safe space for people in our team to be creative, you'll find they will start throwing ideas into the ring. The first may say, "I'm hearing something that starts with an R." Then, vibing off that, the next team member might come in with "Rascally Raspberry," and everyone agrees this could definitely be a hit.

Following the loosely communal structure, ideas begin to bounce about the packaging, ending with a white can with a clean, modern, magenta shape that resembles a rabbit but is not quite a rabbit floating around the can. Perfect! All this coming from a team who has used the best of both worlds—traditional research in conjunction with their sixth sense when they came up with the name. And you were the one who led them to this, being the leader that you are.

Your leadership skills can also be applied to how you can go about increasing your client base. Staying true to your core values and tuning in to what, conceivably, your potential customers want, you can ethically and profitably figure out what you have to offer and send it out to the universe. You can, essentially, lead your future clients on a path directly to you.

## Gain More Clients and Customers

How do you gain more clients? I am not saying you need to reinvent the wheel. I for sure have my own issues when it comes to getting more clients, but having a good product and marketing it heavily is a good start. Possibly most important, however, is the follow-through. Using your intuition, you can manifest more customers by putting it out to the universe. There is more to it, though. You need to first decide what type of clients and customers you want to attract, and then you need to decide if you will retain them or if they will be a one-off client. Then, go after them.

No one wants to throw good money after bad—meaning you don't want to keep spending money the same way if it's not working. We don't want to waste our money marketing to the wrong crowd or trying to sell the wrong thing to the wrong person. This, essentially, is what can happen when you think you know everything or assume you are on top of the game when it comes to why people would want your services.

Let's take my business, for example. The majority of what I do is connect with clients who want psychic readings. I already know that I am able to manifest clients when I put my intuitive magnet to work. However, if I am not consistently doing my manifestation work, the flow of clients dies down pretty quickly. I need to focus on putting my services out for the world to find.

How do I do that? Well, I already know the bulk of my clients want readings, so this is no great mystery. What I've never stopped to consider is the specific "why." I know the basics that everyone wants answers to—relationship, finances, career, family, health, mostly in that order. But I've never really thought of the "why" beyond the obvious. Maybe I should try to use my intuition to find out.

It's about time I tuned in to see the reasons they may want to come in. If I can figure that out, I might be able to change my marketing strategy to attract more people.

### Try This!
### Attracting More Clients

Using my business as an example, imagine wanting to attract more clients. In order to tune in to why they actually would want to come see me over all the other people who offer what I do, we need to see them in their element. This will be easier to do if we can imagine a typical client instead of trying to focus in on 100 different people.

Imagine a woman, midthirties, who wants to come in. We need to ask her questions, and we will write the answers down so we can review them after.

- How soon do you want an appointment?
- What are you hoping to get out of your session?
- What's the number-one question you want answered?
- Why do you want to go in versus letting answers happen on their own?
- What made you reach out to make an appointment?
- Is there anything that jumped out to you that caused you to make an appointment with (insert the name you are using)?
- What else should we know about why you chose to book your appointment?

When you've asked all the questions, go ahead and review your answers. We can do this together. When we asked about time frame, I saw a calendar opened to the next week and no further. That tells me she wants an appointment pretty much right away. When I posed the next question, I heard "answers." This doesn't tell me that much—hopefully the next few will be more detailed. "Is there more out there for me? Please tell me this is not all my life will be" is what I heard for her top concern. I can honestly say I was not expecting that. I thought it would be more like "Should I take the job?" or "Is my deceased boyfriend okay?" This is great. I'm already learning more than I expected. When I tuned in to the next item on the list, I felt her being totally impatient—essentially, I feel like she is just tired of trying to figure things out on her own. "I reached out because I felt warmth from you, and it was easy." Then, "You jumped out at me because I like your cards on Facebook and one of my friends came to see you." Okay, well, this didn't really surprise me. When I asked the final question, I just knew the answer. Desperation and curiosity, it seems, are equally important.

Turns out, if I hadn't utilized my intuition, I probably wouldn't have discovered what was important to my clients and those who aren't clients yet. I know now how to market a bit differently. I can put together some social media posts that play to these sentiments.

For your own business goals, you can come up with any other questions to help you understand how to access and receive more clients or customers. Then market it that way to bring in more traffic. Learning how to appeal to your customer base is huge and can really go a long way toward helping you realize your dreams. I am blessed to do the work that I love, but I need to make a living doing it. I am pretty sure you feel the same way! Drawing in those sales can definitely help.

Once you've brought in the business, you have to learn what makes your customers tick. And although you can remain the leader, you want to be sure that the people you are working with feel important and even special. They need to know you are working for them, and by leading them into the future you are seeing, the rewards will inevitably increase for you both.

# CHAPTER 12

# Create a Comfortable Feeling with Clients, Staff, and Colleagues

*They may forget what you said—*
*but they will never forget how you made them feel.*

—CARL W. BUEHNER

When you're serving others, you're not thinking about yourself. You just let it happen, without questioning it. Sometimes you need to not be the most important person in the room. You need to make others feel like *they're* the center of the universe and you're there to make them comfortable. Reading their energy with your intuitive intelligence allows you to tune in to their level of contentedness, which will translate into success for you and your business. It helps you maintain a connection in an easy, relatable way, whether it's with clients, staff, or even your boss. And take that same energy home with you to create that happy, even cozy, feeling with your family and friends. When you shift your energy to be more attentive, you make people feel significant, and it shows them you value their worth, even when that can be a stretch! Most importantly, it helps generate a trusting atmosphere where people will be more apt to share, explore, and spend!

# Being a Rockstar
# While Not Being the Most Important

Do you know what an oxymoron is? Basically, it's a contradiction in terms, such as "the silence was deafening." It is essentially a juxtaposition of two concepts or words that you wouldn't normally associate with each other. The reason it's important is because you can be powerful while not being the most important person in the room! That sounds counterintuitive, right? It seems like it goes against what being a badass is. However, it can be fundamental in certain circumstances to maintain or establish good connections.

You can be confident; actually, you should be confident. Understanding how to stay excited about what's happening with you and around you keeps you on top. Welcoming other people into your world who are important means you must make room for them and even possibly allow that they have to be the most important in the room currently. It's okay for them to be center stage. They need to be put on a pedestal. The only question, really, is why would you do that? Why would you step back?

You will always be important. As a matter of fact, you will always be number one in your life. However, there are often situations when it's in your best interest to take a back seat. When you need to learn something from someone else, for instance, or when you want to make them feel comfortable. Intuiting how they feel provides you with a direction to go to make them content. When your clients (or staff, boss, coworkers, significant other, or friends) are happy and feel important, they will be more apt to be open to what you want to sell them. Using your gifts can give you data you might not otherwise be privy to, which can afford you a glimpse into what exactly makes them tick. You would be ridiculous to not use that insight when it's readily available to you!

There's no need to limit yourself to only one intuitive sense when you are tuning in to your client. You have a metaphysical cache to draw from, so restricting yourself is not necessary. In fact, it's frowned upon. Making use of all your gifts is key to getting a full picture. The reality is trying to curb your intuition can cause your vibes to slow down and not flow as freely. Allowing all your senses to be open to interpret what you get gives you more insight. Being a success means you use what's available to you.

### *Try This!*
### What Makes Them Tick?

It's a process. You read the energy of people through their handshake back in chapter 3, so you're an old pro at this. You need to take it a step further in order to make that certain someone feel special. The only tricky part is figuring out how to practice doing it. Let's do it with someone you're acquainted with but not too close to. Think of someone you are trying to figure out. It can be a client, a friend—it's totally up to you. You want to decipher what makes them tick. Everyone is different. Happiness comes from many different sources and really depends on the individual. This is what you have to tune in to—what will make them feel content and, more importantly, relaxed. Before you do, make sure you send positive energy out to them and thank them for being open to you. Normally, you don't want to invade someone else's energy, so be grateful you have the opportunity to do this in a humble and respectful manner.

Try opening all your gifts at once. Allowing everything to come through, no matter the sense, can give you a fuller picture. Close your eyes and think of that person. Imagine you can perceive their energy as it streams out of their aura. You may psychically see it, hear it, feel it, or just know it. Take it all in. Do any images come to mind? If so, what are they? Are the images clear? Foggy? Symbolic? Do you hear anything coming through? Sounds? Words? Music? Something you recognize or don't? How about what you feel coming off them? Do you feel their energy? Are you taking on their feelings? Do they feel happy? Sad? Upset? Ecstatic? Nervous? Energized? What kinds of feelings do you get? What else is coming to you? Is there anything you just know? Anything that feels like you know something that you didn't before, seemingly out of nowhere? Let it all sink in as you breathe in and out.

When you feel like you've gotten all you will out of the energy, put it together. What did you perceive? The next level of interpretation is what will generate the most understanding with what you're looking for now. You've utilized all your gifts to discern what you could from their aura. Based on what you've learned, go deeper and see if you can pick up on what might cause them to be happy. Search with all your gifts for a spark, a little light inside them. When you find it, make it bigger, stretch it so you can see what's within it. Read the energy. This is their happy place; the part of their aura that may hold a key to making them at ease. Are the impressions something you can use to determine what would make them relaxed or content? What did you pick up? Process all the impressions you received and figure out if any of it explains to you how you could contribute to making them happy.

## Create That Trusting Atmosphere

It is totally on you to build a supportive foundation for your clients and staff. When you've discovered what makes them happy, you have the ability to increase that level of comfort—for them and of course for you. You want them to be secure with you and what you represent or what you bring to the table. Establish that rapport with them, showing them you know how to make them happy because you've set your sights on them and want them to feel special. There is absolutely nothing wrong with showing respect to them. Your goal is to create a trusting atmosphere so they will want to be with you, buy from you, work for you, and so on.

This doesn't make you or your actions disingenuous. Alternatively, it shows you value them and maybe even have a high opinion of them. Obviously, you want to benefit from your relationship as well. It's a two-way street. Being a success isn't about disregarding others to get ahead. However, recognizing what you can do for someone else and what they may provide you is a great way to exchange energy. So go for it. Show them you appreciate them, and they will, in turn, appreciate you and what you have to offer.

This is not a magic trick—but it is significant when trying to build a relationship. Picking up and deciphering the energy of those you're serving or who are serving you is clearly a considerable part of making the connection. Another step in building that trusting atmosphere, though, is to adjust your own energy. You've worked with your aura. Now is your chance to stretch that aura out in a welcoming and warm way.

Extending your aura for a specific reason can take some practice. Learning how to extend your aura out to other people to create a comfortable vibe is great for every situation. In this specific way you will help generate that trusting atmosphere you are looking for. It's a simple thing you can do that will add to your success.

Erica was having a rough time at work. It was not her ideal job, just something to make money while she finished up college. She was doing the work of three people and gave 100 percent to each one during her shifts, so after a staff meeting when her manager pulled her to the side to talk, she was surprised.

"Do you want to work here, Erica? It doesn't seem like you want to be here," she said.

"Ummm, excuse me?" Erica responded, her jaw on the floor.

"You need to work harder. It doesn't seem like you're putting in any effort. I don't think you want to be here."

Erica went home very upset. She was working so hard that she had to wear short-sleeve shirts even though it was winter because she was sweating like she was at the gym. She didn't understand what was happening or why she was being admonished since she was giving it her all. She felt so disrespected and disenchanted that she wanted to put in her two weeks' notice right away. I told her to wait and think about what was happening.

She knew, and I believed, that she truly was putting in the effort. What else could have triggered this? Why had she been singled out? I questioned whether it was because the manager wasn't personally feeling the love from Erica. It seemed to me that if she were able to send some warm energy out to her manager, things would turn around. I knew it would probably be difficult. Not only was she upset, but she was mad. She was positive that what was happening to her was wrong and she didn't want to give them any more effort, but she also wanted to make money. She decided to try staying at least until she could get another job. In order to do that she needed to make a few adjustments, the first being what I suggested.

I explained she could send positive, warm energy to her manager. Tuning in to her aura, she could focus on loving energy. Then she should imagine pushing it out in waves, kind of like ripples on a pond. Once she could feel the energy flowing outward, she could direct it specifically toward her manager. When I send positive energy out, it helps me to visualize it. I envision sparkly, glittery streams of energy meandering and pulsing their way out into the world. Erica was able to do this as well and felt like it reached her boss.

The next day, she was stressed about going into work. When she arrived, the manager looked a bit confused, partly due to the fact that she really expected Erica to give up and quit and partly, I definitely believe, because her feelings toward Erica had changed, for no reason she could put her finger on. But we knew. The day passed by with Erica working hard as usual. By the end of the day, the manager was pleasant and even, almost, friendly. Erica could tell her manager had no idea what had happened, but she seemed pleased, for the first time, with Erica. Erica, in turn, felt empowered. She was now (almost!) excited to go to work and bring her vivacious, happy attitude along with her.

This is what I'm talking about—changing the atmosphere around you by expanding your energy and sending it out toward the people you are hoping to connect with. I'm not telling you to invade someone else's energy. That would be totally unethical. However, when you are doing it in a positive way, trying to create a mutually beneficial relationship, it is okay. Clearly, it is not altogether philanthropic or altruistic—you want something from it. Building that trust between you, though, is a great reason to link up.

Whether it's to land a business deal, keep your staff happy, or create a better environment at home, creating that comfortable feeling is critical. You won't get anything from anyone if there is no trust. Neither will you be happy without respect. Putting someone else on the pedestal and making them feel important brings out the best in them. Shifting your energy and, yes, letting go of your ego, shows them you value them and their position with you. Using your metaphysical gifts to reach out to them and experience their feelings as well as sending them your positive energy will make for a more content association all around, which will leave you feeling like a total rockstar and add to your success.

## When Their Energy Has You Questioning Your Intuition

We work so hard to make everything come together and create an atmosphere that caters to others while making us feel good. Whether it's business or pleasure, this usually has us on a path toward success. It, however, is not always about getting others to trust us, and creating that comfortable mood for everyone else. We also have to pay attention to how we feel when working or playing with other people. Back in chapter 4 we talked about picking up the vibes from others, specifically their handshakes. Building that trust so others can have confidence in us is one thing—being sure we expect and have that same trust in the people we are doing business with is critical. You don't want to mess around, on any level, with someone you don't believe or have confidence in.

Heather Hansen O'Neill, a business coach, author, and prominent speaker, was not someone who regularly tuned in to her intuition—until she had no other choice. She told me of the situation that made her a huge believer in her gifts.

When I asked her of her intuitive experiences, she told me, "I will never ignore my intuition again. There have been numerous small occasions when my intuition has attempted to guide me. It's the joyful voice that has led me to the best relationships, the activities that have made my heart sing, and the encouragement that has kept me going when I've been down. It's also the quiet voice that questions someone or something that doesn't feel right. I've noticed that when I haven't listened to the voice, I've been disappointed with the outcome. But no time more than in the following situation."

Turns out, in the very first conversation with a particular man she met, caution bells were ringing in her mind. However, she really liked the offer he was making to do some business together, so she ignored it.

Heather dove into this business relationship knowing this man prided himself on his outstanding sales ability. Every time they had a call, her voice of intuition would whisper, "Something's not right," but she didn't listen because on paper the deal seemed solid.

As time wore on, the situation worsened. More and more often their opinions clashed, and she found him saying and doing things that were in blatant conflict with her character, and the things she believed in her heart to be true.

She went on to tell me that in these moments the voice practically hissed at her to listen. Still, she didn't listen because by this point, she was involved and she didn't want to disappoint the people they were supposed to be helping. When she would question him, he poured on the charm and made her wonder if she had perhaps been wrong. His tone was cajoling and very convincing.

It bothered Heather so much she wasn't sleeping well. She started to feel physically ill anytime she spoke with him. She couldn't even think of him without anger welling up. During one particular call, he turned the conversation around and blamed her for something he had done. It was then she realized the extent of his narcissism.

Heather said her inner voice shouted, "Get out!"

She finally paid attention and severed all ties with him. The relief she felt in that instant was incredibly freeing. Only later did Heather find out about the other people he had deceived. Many people came forward and told her that he had tricked them too.

She told me, "Now I am filled with gratitude for my inner voice, my intuition, and use it to guide me in business and in life. It's a powerful tool that I trust!"

Sometimes, as with Heather's situation, it takes a while to really trust your gut instincts. That whispered guidance can often feel like your imagination. Trusting your intuition goes a long way toward trusting your business and personal relationships and situations. We often sense caution flags waving, but our desires can shut them down, allowing our wants to overrule them. When we do this, we are usually setting ourselves up for failure in one way or the other. In this type of situation, almost more than ever, we must pay attention to what our metaphysical senses are telling us.

It's crucial to make other people comfortable. One of the key components to doing that is tuning in to the energy of the person you are with to determine what makes them happy. It's okay to put others on a pedestal, but not to your detriment. Creating a trusting environment for both them and you is also a critical piece of what's necessary to make you both successful. Knowing, though, when the person you are trying to impress isn't trustworthy makes it that much more important to trust your gut instincts and run, run as far away from that person as you can. When you can build a positive environment for all to be successful and are careful whom you trust, you will really thrive.

# CHAPTER 13

# Bring Out Positivity
# for Success

*[A nemesis is] often someone who is doing what we would secretly like to.
Or perhaps they appear to be living their life in a way that we aspire to.*

—HONEY LANCASTER JAMES

Haters gonna hate. When they throw shade at you, do you need to respond? You are filled with positivity that you can excavate and use, even with the shadiest people. Sometimes you must really dig down deep in order to bring that good energy up, but that produces a stronger foundation with which to build yourself and everyone else up. When you do that, it helps pull out the constructive and positive attributes in the people you are dealing with. When you make use of this, you can all be successful, and isn't that what you want? Leave the haters home or hit them with so much damn positivity that they can't help but convert.

So what's this negativity about? Why would haters go out of their way to try and put you down? It could be any number of things. Possibly, they are jealous of who you are and what you have to offer. Maybe it goes deeper and you've struck a chord with them in some way. Perhaps they are just so miserable they want everyone to be miserable too. But maybe there's a different reason, and it might be a good idea to try to discern it.

Truthfully, sometimes it's easier to sink down into the depths of despair over simple things than to figure out how to make something work. Focusing on positivity instead can produce a more successful outcome. Instead of tearing others down, build them up! Bringing positive energy into the mix can convert even your biggest opposition, which in turn can bring everyone together. This creates a successful outcome, which is obviously what you want in business and in your personal life. Whether it's difficult to do or easy really depends on how much you are willing to forgo the negative arguments, release your ego, and mix it up in a different, more productive way.

Letting go of your ego does not, in any way, make you less powerful. As a matter of fact, it increases your success because it proves you can do whatever it takes to make your client, partner, or even spouse feel like they are the most important person in the room. It is always valuable to discover what is important to others to show them they and their opinions matter.

## Responding for Success

Normally, our responses to negativity can run the gamut from getting angry to ignoring the person who is throwing the shade your way. What's the best option for you? You can choose the angry comeback, but what will that get you? You can ignore them. That might bring you a moment of respite, but then what? The haters are going to keep on hating. So often they are sending out a reflection of what they need to deal with themselves. What else can you do? Respond with positivity.

People who are successful don't need to put others down. If the person you're dealing with is ragging on you, there is probably a reason within themselves. Instead of taking what they are saying or doing personally, you can use your intuition to figure out where it is coming from. Tune in to their energy and ask questions: Where is this coming from? What do they see in me that they don't like in themselves? Are they responding to something I'm doing that bothers them? Is there something going on in their life right now that's causing them distress? Do they need help with a situation? Are they stressing out about something specific? These are just a few. Ask your intuition for any additional questions that may assist in deciphering what is happening with them.

Now you need to respond in kind. No, really. In *kind-ness*. In order to break the cycle and bring out the positive attributes in people, you have to give them some kind of antidote to their life issue. This isn't your first rodeo—you've tuned in to your intuition before.

After you've interpreted what you think their issue is, the problem then becomes what to do with it. You have a couple of options, but here's one. Send them energy, clearing energy specific to them. Based on what you've discovered, you want to improve their mood and, by extension, their attitude toward you. By envisioning what you intuited was wrong, causing them to throw shade your way, you can work on lightening it up for them. Imagine taking the source of their bitterness and putting it in a box. Tape up the box. Wrap it up with string. Send it air mail into the universe. Finally, send them positive energy—let it pulse from you to them. Keep doing it as long as necessary to feel you made a difference.

You're responding to their actions or words by alleviating some of their stress. Your intention is really what's important. Not only are you trying to clear their negative action toward you, you are responding with encouragement. You're able to let go of your ego long enough to think about what they need. That alone will help you bring out the positive attributes in you both and get you that much closer to success.

## Check In with Yourself and Learn

There is more than one way to skin a cat, or so they say. I personally don't ever want to skin anything. There is, though, more than one way to handle someone's negativity. It will definitely require you to put your ego on the back burner and open yourself up. It also may take a lot of soul searching for it to work.

Most criticisms are born of mirroring. Many times what someone is attacking you about is just a reflection of their own self. Though it may be annoying, it's not all about you. However, there is sometimes a basis in truth.

What they are seeing in you might just be something you should consider looking at yourself. This takes a strong spirit to admit you have something others don't like, but once you're able to realize it, you also realize not everyone is going to appreciate you, and that's okay. Rather than getting angry or resisting, use it to your advantage and look deeper.

Think about what they are saying. Does it resonate with you? Do you understand what they are saying or where they are coming from? If so, it can make it that much easier to consider their feedback with gratitude. Appreciate the critique, even if it wasn't sent out of love, and be grateful they helped you apprehend it, especially if it's something that you probably would not have become aware of.

Return their feedback with some of your own—thank them for their candor and let them know it is because of this that you're able to humbly contemplate that part of what you're doing. You're intelligent enough to know that what they said may not hold any merit whatsoever, but it still afforded you the opportunity to become conscious of things you may change. Again, express to them, through your words or actions, how their comments have created a soul searching and that you welcome any further explanation about what they said. By allowing your ego to step out of the way, you've made room for your spirit to explore what you, maybe, could do differently. By validating them, you are valuing each other, and this will only add to your success.

## Fuel Your Fire with Criticism

Sometimes it is just about you. It's not about trying to figure out the why behind what the naysayer said or did. That doesn't really matter when you handle their criticism in this way. What does matter is what you choose to do about it. Again, there are so many different directions you can go when someone is throwing shade at you. This one, you might find, suits your personality better.

Instead of letting it shut you down, take their criticism as a challenge. They are, in a way, helping you prepare for your future. Think about what they are saying—does it make sense? Is it something that you've thought about in the past? Now that you've figured out how it relates to you, take the opportunity to do something about it. Instead of letting it make you feel iced out, let it fuel your fire. Don't get all niggly about it. Rather, allow it to fan the flames to your passion.

Decide for yourself that you want to show them they're wrong. You want to build up your strengths and show them how incredible you can be. Take their disparaging comments and let them prompt you to build up your potency in that area. Turn the kryptonite they are throwing at you into your power. Prove to yourself and everyone else just how amazing you are! Develop your tools and grow your gifts, and you will become even more confident and demonstrate to others that you are not too full of yourself to make some needed adjustments. Thank the original person for helping stimulate you into doing something.

## Turn It into a Conversation, Not an Argument

How cool would you be if you could turn criticism around and make it into a conversation instead of an argument? Instead of rebelling against the other person, how about you bring them into the dialogue? What is it about you that they criticized? Is it something you can discuss? Is it rooted in feelings of inadequacy, either on their part or yours? Have the talk with them—tell them you want to discuss how they feel because it is important to you. Most will not expect this, and the surprise will intrigue them.

In general, people are naturally skeptical of new ideas. Possibly this has something to do with the naysaying. If so, perfect! Have a discussion about what you are trying to accomplish or what you are trying to do. While you have the conversation, send them positive energy. It will make them feel more at ease and decrease the energetic distance between you.

If it's due to them being reluctant to understand, bring them to the wild side. Explain what it is you want to achieve and why you think it would work. Share with them, in a different way, what you are doing and why. Essentially, you need to help them comprehend the situation so they will feel connected to what you are selling, sharing, or explaining. Once you both grasp the concepts, the positive energy will rise. Remember, just like the skeptical person, send positive energy as you're explaining! It will help them get a handle on what's happening.

There are so many different ways to convert the negatives to positives. You might resonate with one method over the other. The options in this section are just a smattering of ideas, but they can all get the juices flowing and sway people to be constructive rather than critical. You've set about to be successful—don't let the haters change that. Instead, change them! Bringing out their positive attributes enables you to increase your presence and your positivity, which inevitably sets you well on your way to success and, obviously, makes you even more commanding!

## Determine What Matters Most
## to Your Client, Staff, and Even Nemesis

Trying to figure out what everyone wants can be a difficult task, especially when you are working so hard to give off the air of a self-reliant person at the same time. You don't always want to ask. Using your intuition can bring you to that extra level of understanding. Determining what matters most expresses to your clients just how important you think they are. And, let's face it, everyone wants to feel special. The reality is determining what matters can give you an in. Your client has an idea of what is foremost on their wish list. Your staff also know what they are looking for. Even your rivals have an idea about what is essential for them.

What do your clients need to feel secure? Clients are definitely different from your staff or your competition. You need to determine what is key to their success and happiness. What do they want? Whatever it is, it has to matter to them. It could be something they don't even know they want ... yet. How are you going to figure it out? The answer isn't as simple as you think it may be—it's a combination of things. The first approach is to use your physical senses to suss them out. You must pay attention to what they say and do. Are they sharing the basics with you? Listen to what they're saying. What are their goals? What do they want to accomplish? What are their hopes and fears? The next approach is to use your intuition, of course. Tune in to figure out what matters.

## Try This!
## What's Imperative to Your Clients?

Imagine you are looking at a blank canvas. Really see it in your mind's eye. Let the size of it, the edges, and the texture show up. Take an imaginary paint brush and paint everything you picked up on physically, filling in all the details. Take a step back and check out what you've painted. Does it make sense in your rational mind? Do you see the details with greater clarity than you did before you painted your picture?

Now it's time to get metaphysical. Tune in to your client's energy. Grab your paintbrush again and another blank canvas. What do you think your client's aspirations are? What is their endgame? What's important to them? Start painting what you pick up—concentrate on the simple as well as the complex. What happens when you focus on the general principles as well as the details of what matters to them? Does it change what you get? Do you get different vibes when you pay attention to different aspects of your client? Use all your intuitive senses to help you paint a complete picture.

Blend the two pictures together now. Do you see what matters most to your client? Are you able to gain a deeper understanding of what is top on their list of wants? Can you feel, from your painting, what motivates them? What is at the core of their desires? Can you summarize, easily, what is most important? Think about this for a minute.

Determining what matters to your client is important in many ways—it lets your client know you value them and care about their needs. It also tells them you are willing to go the extra mile to determine what key components they need to be satisfied with your services. This is not about the sales, though ultimately that is your goal.

This is more about building a rapport with them. It is about building a relationship in which they feel like they can trust you. So what do you do with all the information you gleaned from your painting? You present it to them. You communicate to them and show them you know what is important to them.

I received an email from a client last week. He had copied and pasted a rates and payments section of my website that advertised hypno-coaching, past-life regression, and mentoring. It mentioned nothing of a reading.

"Hi. I want to come in to see you," he wrote.

"Okay, fantastic! What service would you like to schedule?" I responded back to him.

"Well, what do you suggest?"

Now, I was paying attention to the words he had copied. I felt out of the three different services, the past-life regression was talking to me the strongest, though I still wasn't convinced. I emailed him back.

"Would you like to do a past-life regression?"

"Sure, whatever you think," he emailed back.

Honestly, people pay a pretty penny to come in. They pretty much always know what they want. This particular client was a bit of a mystery. Something still didn't feel right, so I messaged him again.

"I know you said yes to a past-life regression, but I am feeling like a reading would better suit your needs. I think this is more what you want. I feel like the information that comes through will give you a more fulfilling experience."

"Great. I'll see you soon!"

There was no argument and no response either way that I had changed his appointment to a psychic reading. I must admit I was a bit nervous. I wanted to be sure he would have an appointment that would make sense—I wanted it to matter to him, and it didn't seem like it did.

When he came into the office, I said, "I hope it's okay that we are doing a reading today? I feel like that will provide you with the most benefits."

"I have to say, I was open to the other stuff. When you suggested a past-life regression session, I was kind of like, okay. But I was really hoping for a reading, so I am so glad you changed your mind and gave me what I wanted."

I have no idea why he didn't just tell me that from the beginning. I think he was deferring to me, as the expert, to determine what he needed. Even though I had never spoken to him or talked to him about what he was looking for in the past, it seemed to resonate more with him to let me decide. Luckily, I went with my gut instincts, my intuitive senses, and felt that to provide him with anything other than a reading would have left him somewhat dissatisfied. I was right, and when he walked out the door, he was happy—not only with his reading, but also with the fact that I had picked up on what mattered to him most.

It really makes no difference what the situation is. Having your clients realize you value what matters to them makes the service or product you are providing them that much better. When you use your gifts, you are unapologetically performing at your best.

## What Your Staff Wants

Sometimes people disregard what their employees want or need. There can be a feeling of "I'm the boss, so whatever I say goes." However, the good bosses really take into consideration how their staff feels and what matters to them. Disregarding their wants and needs will make them believe you don't care. When you don't care about someone, what's going to happen? They will either just walk away, or they won't give you 100 percent. When you treat them badly, they will feel bad. Plain and simple. They will hold back and may even be afraid. Above all, they won't feel any loyalty toward you. Why would they?

How can you remedy that? The first step would be to show them some respect. Letting them know that what matters to them is important to you is a wonderful way to express that. Telling them is fantastic—showing them is even better. In order to do this, you must pick up on the clues. When it's your staff, it's okay to ask them what's important to them. Tuning in with your intuition can bring your understanding to the next level.

Go deeper. After you've asked your staff what they want, look further. Use your abilities to concentrate on what is behind what they want. For example, if they tell you they want flexible hours, intuit why. Is it because they have another job because they are not making enough working with you? Is it because they are having a hard time with childcare? Is it because they want to travel? You can ask, but they may not feel comfortable enough to tell you.

Is there something they are doing that is causing you grief? If so, what is it? When I was the controller of a company, I had an office staff that included a front desk employee. This was an important job because they also answered the phones and they were the first in line with our customers. This employee was someone I had hired, and I chose him over others because I felt he needed some help.

The problem came a few months later when he started coming to work late. Every morning, just a bit later. At first it was just five minutes, then ten, then fifteen. We needed someone who showed up, pleasantly, on time every day. I had to talk to him. At first it was essentially me giving him the ultimatum—get here or you're fired. Then I decided to tune in and take it further.

I picked up on some trouble at home. I was tuning in to cash flow as well as transportation. I felt the money crunch and I saw, symbolically, a street sign with a school on it, with wheels rolling down the road. I asked him about it.

"What is going on at home? I feel like you're having some issues with money and transportation? Is there something wrong with your car?" I questioned.

"Umm, my mother's car broke down, and we don't have the money to fix it. She is saving up now, but mine is the only working car and we have to get my little brother to school. My sister needs my car to get to her job as well.

It's just been hard trying to get everyone moving so I can get here on time. I will tell them that we have to change something because I obviously can't afford to lose this job," he answered honestly.

Of course. I could feel there was something deeper than him just being lazy or oversleeping. In fact, he was working really hard to help take care of his family. Because I used my intuition to determine what was going on, I was able to come up with a temporary solution to help him until the family was able to fix their other car. I happened to know one of his coworkers lived near him, so I asked if there was a way he could hitch a ride for the next couple of weeks. They both got to work on time and even developed a strong friendship. If I hadn't gone deeper into what was happening, he would have lost his job. It is these types of moments that show your staff you care, and you want them to be successful.

## Why Would You Want Your Nemesis to Succeed?

We measure ourselves against our nemesis. That sounds strange, doesn't it? But it's true. When we have someone whom we don't get along with, we might simply ignore them or stay away from them. Alternatively, a nemesis can spur us on, make us want to work harder or be better so we can best them. I know, we are all about self-actualization. We should want to succeed to better ourselves for the sake of fueling our own sense of self with our personal accomplishments. However, let's get real. Despite your feelings of animosity toward a nemesis and their business dealings, you may also kind of secretly respect them. They are someone who in another lifetime might be your best friend. They are like your mirror, not only showing you what you don't want but also reflecting back qualities you want for yourself.

Your nemesis needs to succeed because if they do, you know you can too. You don't need to measure your successes against theirs, but there is an intrinsic value in healthy competition. When you can help your nemesis succeed, even if they are not aware of your generosity, it increases your own chances of getting ahead.

On another level, there's something about your nemesis that attracts you to their energy. It's almost as though they give off a pheromone that pulls you in. Your energy is sucked toward theirs, and the only way to get it back is to work harder. The petty rivalry you've developed is not fueled by hate but competition. If you can tune in to their energy, without getting stuck in it, it can help you intuitively know what to do to help lead you to success. When your nemesis succeeds and you're attached and tuned in, the pathway to your own success becomes clearer because you're able to kind of ride their wave, and it elevates your own energy.

Understanding what's important to the people who are part of your circle, from friend to foe, provides you an opportunity to get ahead. As you've learned, it's not just about learning from your boss or your client. You also realize that understanding what drives your staff and even your nemesis can play a significant role in your own business or personal growth. Speaking of growth, hiring the right people from the start to help expand your productivity is crucial. Learning to tune in to your intuition during interviews and reviews as both the employee and the employer can help you secure your future achievements.

# CHAPTER 14

# Trust Your Intuition during Interviews and Reviews and when Hiring

*Intuition is indeed a part of your life,*
*and you don't want to separate your values and principles from it.*

—DIANE BRANDON, *INTUITION FOR BEGINNERS*

If only you had someone in your ear, telling you what to say and do while you are in an interview or performing or even receiving a review, who could show the other people that you know what you're doing. It's too bad you don't have that. Oh, wait—you do! It's your intuition. Learning to trust that your intuitive instincts will guide you during important events such as interviews goes a long way toward relaxing you and making you feel comfortable enough to get the job, or even to read the other person to see if they're worthy of hiring.

Being interviewed can be nerve-racking. It can cause a lot of stress for a multitude of reasons. If you are in desperate need of a job, the interview process can be intimidating. When you are hoping for a specific position or a job at a specific company, it can make you very nervous. There can be a great longing for the potential employer to like you and respect you. If your plan is to move across the country, finding the perfect fit by using your intuition can be critical, so you need to be sure.

## Multiple Interviews

Brei is a badass lawyer. She was living in Washington, DC, and decided she wanted to look for a new job to mix things up a bit. She sent her resume to a bunch of different companies across the United States. She had a variety of interviews set up. She physically went to a few and had video interviews with a few others. She received a great offer from a company that she decided to accept, so she cancelled any remaining meetings with other firms. She was pretty confident she'd found a good fit.

Then, she realized a video interview had snuck its way in, without her realizing, for a company out in California. It was for in-house legal counsel for a biotech firm, and she figured, "What the heck. I don't have to do anything but talk to them for a little bit," so she kept the online appointment. Brei met with them, by computer, knowing full well she had already accepted an offer at a different firm—a good offer at that. She would be making great money and it was an easy move, so she wasn't sure why she had decided on keeping the interview, except that it felt like something was pulling her toward this new company. They called her back and flew her out to California to have a formal interview. All the while, she knew she had already verbally accepted a different offer.

Still, not sure why she was doing it, she met with the biotech firm. Immediately, she felt a sense of community. They had a vibe that she had picked up on from the first interview and she loved it. She told the company that if they wanted her, they would have to make an offer quickly because she literally had movers lined up to get her in a new place for the other position.

They sent their proposal, which Brei decided immediately to accept. Right out of the gate it turned out to be more money with greater benefits. That was just the beginning, though. When she started her new job in San Francisco, she began realizing what else she had jumped on board for and she absolutely loved it. The culture there was phenomenal. They truly cared about their employees. They had special scheduled employee retreat days and meditation moments. They were constantly offering events and fun things for the staff and everyone from the janitors to the vice presidents were treated with respect and kindness. The basic mission of the company was to value the patient for whom they were trying to develop new treatment plans (they focus on rare medical conditions), and that shined through in every step of the way.

Brei had trusted her intuition during the interview process. She had decided to listen to her intuition and keep her interview even after she had already decided on somewhere else because it just felt like it would be a good idea. She is so happy she did. She loves her new job and recognizes that if she hadn't used her intuitive gifts to explore her options further, she probably would not have been nearly as happy.

You utilize almost all your physical senses: sight to see how they present physically, touch during the initial handshake, listening to them with your hearing, and definitely your sense of smell to be sure they are not obnoxiously stinky! (I'm pretty sure you don't want to taste them, but that may be a whole other career.) So now, of course you'd want to enhance those physical senses with your metaphysical senses—you will garner so much more information from them besides what they are telling you.

## Reviews

Reviews are very similar to interviews—you want to impress the boss and you want to keep your job. It's an opportunity for a promotion or to apply for a different position. When you are the one giving the review, it's a good idea to tune in to the energy of the employee before they come in. If you need to get more out of them, it's best to understand what motivates them. If you are the one getting the evaluation, you need to read the situation. First of all, is it going to be positive? If so, what can you try to get out of it? Do you want to just be happy with the positive feedback, or do you want to ask for a raise or some type of advancement? If the read you get is negative, what should your response be? Would it behoove you to still ask for what you want, or should you be thankful if you walk out of there with a job? Either way, your intuition can impact your review, whether you are the one giving it or getting it.

Jen was a long-time employee at a cable company, which was twenty minutes away from her home. During her review, a positive one, she was asked to step up to lead a team at a higher level. It sounded great to her until she heard where she'd be working. Apparently, the position was an hour and a half commute each way. She had some thinking to do.

Jen decided to tune in to her intuition before she agreed to take the job. There were definitely some benefits—she would make more money, for starters. She would be team leader to not just one team, but two. The only downside was that commute. Who wants to drive that far every day? Not too many people deem it worth the distance. Jen didn't either.

For some reason, though, Jen still felt drawn to the position. She was feeling like something would change with the commute if she were to take the job. She listened to her intuition and told her boss she would gladly accept the offer, but if there was a possibility to move her home base closer to where she lived to shorten her commute, she would greatly appreciate it.

Wouldn't you know it, after Jen trusted her intuition and took the job as team leader, they told her she would only have to wait about two months because they had just procured a new space and they were building it out. When Jen asked if she could house at least one of her teams in the new location as well, her boss responded that not only would they give her the one team there, but she could move both teams.

The benefits outweighed the potential downside. If she hadn't tuned in to her vibes, she wouldn't have trusted that it would work out. Jen would still be stuck in her previous position, no raise, no promotion, no new team to supervise. By having faith that her intuition was showing her the right career path, she was headed toward success and proved what an asset she is, to herself and her boss.

## Hiring

When you are a boss, in any sense of the word, that means you have at least one employee. Hiring that one employee can be the single most important decision you make. It literally can make your business or break it. That's why it's so essential to tune in to your vibes to figure out who the potential hire really is, beyond what they are showing you physically.

You can get extremely detailed in your résumé searching, preferring to look for someone who meets the exact criteria you think you want for the position. Or you can choose to be a bit more flexible, coupled with your own intuition to determine who might be the best fit. Being perfect on paper doesn't mean you will work well together. The quality of the person and not necessarily just their work skills should play a role in determining if they might be beneficial. That, again, is one great reason to use your intuition.

Some years ago, Carol owned a boutique. She was pretty much a solo act, but she was getting older and knew she wanted to be able to take some time off. In order to do that, she needed to hire someone to work the boutique. She took an ad out in the local paper outlining the basic job requirements and waited.

She ended up with three applicants. Carol set up interviews with all of them individually. The first one was a woman named Jane who was in her forties and had managed a store previously. She had experience dealing with the ins and outs of running a place, and she claimed to run a tight ship. She told Carol she was up to the challenge of making the boutique better, and as a matter of fact, she already had plans to rearrange some things and move a few racks of inventory around.

The second applicant was a bit younger, in her thirties. Arlene had never run a store, but she had been an office manager. She was used to being in charge and making decisions. She was nice enough and had a bit of a rough edge to her but seemed perfectly capable. On paper, she was a pretty good fit. She was eager to take over from Carol and was ready to start immediately.

The third applicant was in her late twenties, a nice young woman. Stacy had worked at a daycare for a few years and then nannied for a couple of different families. She'd had a scattering of retail experience while she was in school. She was looking to transition into a different type of job. She was excited for the opportunity to learn the business and seemed enthusiastic to meet and deal with the customers.

This boutique was Carol's baby. She had built it from scratch into a thriving downtown business. She nurtured it into what it was and knew most of the customers by name. She was not retiring, but she did need some help, so she had to decide soon. Previously, the only employees Carol had were temporary—high school students during the holiday season. This time, she had to make a choice for a more permanent, full-time position.

Carol considered the first applicant, Jane. She already had experience and was eager to get in and begin making changes. Carol tried tuning in to her intuition about this one and essentially just felt a flat, kind of empty energy. She tried to feel the connection she might have to Carol's customers and she couldn't. Not that she expected to, but she figured she'd give it a go.

She moved on to number two, Arlene. Again, she had experience being in charge—she knew how to run a place and make it more efficient. When Carol tapped into the second person's energy, she felt an edge. It almost felt hard to her. When she tried to zone in on the relationship with the boutique customers, it felt almost detached, like Arlene kind of didn't bond with them at all.

Then it was time to consider the third person, Stacy. She had minimal experience, but right off the bat Carol loved that she worked with kids. She linked into this young woman's energy and immediately felt a warm sensation. She wasn't sure what it meant, but it felt good. Then, as she had with the others, she tried to imagine what the rapport would be like with the customers and saw Stacy laughing with the current and new customers, and even got an image of her talking baby talk to one customer's kids.

Carol knew, though she was the least qualified, that the third one was a charm. She offered Stacy the position and she accepted—and even better than that, she never left. Carol had listened to her intuition and chosen the woman who felt the best and was still glad she had. Carol received numerous compliments on her employee, and she felt perfectly comfortable leaving the store and letting her run it. If she had based her decision solely on experience, she never would have picked Stacy.

Carol used her intuition to choose her employee. She didn't have any regrets. Whether you are hiring, attending an interview, giving a review, or getting a review, paying attention to and even searching for what your metaphysical senses are telling you are key. It's so important, not only for your business but also your personal success, to tune in to your money-making intuitive senses. Carol focused in on what was important for the future of the store. It only follows that your sales will increase. You've got the right people in place; the next logical action is understanding how marketing what you're creating can take you to the next level.

# CHAPTER 15

# Better Utilize Your Instincts for Sales and Marketing

*Intuition is used not just to target data, but to actually interpret*
*it for greater significance and reachability,*
*intuiting the moment at which the emotions and subconscious*
*of the consumer is most receptive.*

—RICK SNYDER

Even though the days of door-to-door salesmen are almost obsolete, sales and marketing are not. Getting your product or service out to where it needs to go is a vital part of any business. Here's the thing, though: if it were easy, everyone would be rich! And we all know that being successful is critical to feeling empowered in business. This is where your intuitive gifts come into play. You can really utilize your ability to tune in and decide what type of promotion you need to focus on or marketing you need.

## Creative Intuition

When we access our creativity, we are opening our intuition. They are both part of the right brain. The right brain is the more creative, intuitive, and somewhat colorful side, while the left brain is more analytical, linear, and logic based. Artists and those who have more of a right-brained slant will often access their intuition by channeling it. Marketing and sales strategists gain inspiration through their creativity. Taking it a step further, they will do well to use their intuitive senses for developing a plan to market their product.

The best marketing strategies don't necessarily even sell a product, but they offer a brand. They are able to tap into the general population, or even a niche market, depending upon what the product is, to determine what would impress them or attract them to the product. Think for a moment about car sales. Yes, they show the product, but habitually, what they are selling you is the idea of freedom and fun. They show you open roads, excitement, and sexy people. They know what we want and aren't afraid to give it to us.

We already know intuition is an intrinsic and natural part of who we are. It adds value to everything we do. It lends itself to our creativity and provides us with an ever-evolving wisdom, which is exactly what we need to formulate strategies to sell products.

## *Try This!*
## Tune In to See the Plan

So how do you do it? You use your intuition, of course. Your instincts are available and should be heavily relied upon. Imagine you have a business that needs marketing. Let's pretend it's a new organic coffee shop. There's a lot of competition out there, so how would you conceive the marketing plan? Tune in and ask the necessary questions.

First, let's think about it rationally. A coffee shop. There are so many out there already, so what makes this one stand out? It is organic, so we can play up that aspect. We are not, however, going to tell the public that it's organic by just saying it. We have to make them want it. What or who do we want to provide with organic food and drink? Babies. Yup, that's right, I said babies. Obviously, we are not selling to babies, and we are not trying to convince babies to drink coffee, but we want our babies to be healthy and we associate organic with healthy. So let's play to that. We will talk about how in a minute.

There's another option, though. What about pets? People love happy, bouncy puppies—especially when they are playing with babies. Now there are two different marketing aspects we can utilize, but we are not yet sure how. Once we've gotten to this point, it's time to use our intuitive intelligence.

Are we going to use babies and puppies? Or just one or the other? The primary basis of the marketing will be based on this concept, so we need to tune in. Close your eyes for a moment. Think about your different intuitive gifts—clairvoyance, clairaudience, clairsentience, and claircognizance. Ask the following questions, and one by one, tune in to each of your senses.

- How old should the baby be?
- Should the baby be a boy or girl?
- Where should the baby be? Stroller? Highchair? Baby backpack on the front or back of Mom or Dad?
- Who should baby be there with? Mom, Dad, friends, bunch of moms? Other babies? Other kids?
- Should there be a puppy? How big? What kind? What color?
- Where should they be? In the shop? Walking down the street in front of the shop? With a cup of coffee?
- Where should the dog be? Waiting outside? Looking into the coffee shop?
- Should they be drinking the coffee? Ordering coffee? Eating a snack?
- Should they be talking? Laughing? Smiling?

Once you've tuned in to your different senses and asked all the questions, think about how each of the senses responded and write down your perceptions. Did you get the same answers with each sense? Or different ones? Did your answers make sense? What did they tell you?

Now, look at what you've intuited. This is the beginning of your marketing plan. By merging your intuition with your traditional marketing ideas, you will utilize all your data together. You are integrating both sides of your brain—the analytical/logical as well as the creative/intuitive. This is how you will develop an incredible marketing plan.

You have this organic coffee shop. And the marketing shows a happy puppy waiting outside with a father, while the mother and the stroller-bound laughing baby bring the coffee and some cookies out to the father, as well as a doggy treat—all organic and all together. They walk into the park, in the sunshine, filled with laughter, smiles, a kiss from the mom to the dad, and a wet puppy kiss to the baby, who laughs as she holds up her organic cookie. Now that's a great advertisement.

Tuning in to figure out how to market your product or your business can help you not only increase sales but also become a leader in your niche. The integration of intuitive vibes and logical thought make for a great partnership. It can get you exactly where you need to be. No matter what the product, you can create different circumstances and ask the questions, based on the fundamental ideas.

## Try This!
## Marketing on the Fly

You've done the deep, straightforward marketing strategy—creating the plan. But how about an even easier way? Somewhat similar to the previous exercise, this time it's a quick, on-the-fly, uncomplicated approach. You've asked the questions and tuned in slowly, with great thought. The key to this method is to tap into your intuition without thinking about it. The first thing that comes to mind is what your answer is—don't judge it, don't question it, just trust it. It's easy.

Before you do anything, bring yourself to a meditative state. Slow yourself down. Breathe in and feel relaxation begin to fill up your body as the oxygen spreads. As you breathe out, release any tension you still have in your body. Then, inhale again. Breathe in the belief that you will easily tune in to your metaphysical senses. As you exhale, imagine breathing out any doubt that you will connect to your intuition. Continue until you are totally relaxed, tuned in, and ready to begin.

Now, here's the gist of it: think of your problem, dilemma, or question and then just state it in your mind or out loud. Immediately after that, write down the impressions you receive from the universe. Then, evaluate what you've recorded. Remember, don't deliberate. Keep it simple.

*Problem:* What would be a good product to bring to market?
*Answer:* Jellybeans, stuffed animals, Easter baskets, children.
*Evaluation:* A good product at this time would have something to do with Easter and would appeal to children.

We've got the basics. We need to home in further to get more details.

*Problem:* What Easter product for children should we bring to market?
*Answer:* Soft, jellybeans, game, cheap.
*Evaluation:* Create an inexpensive game with stuffed fake jellybeans that we can market to children for their Easter baskets.

We've taken it a bit further, and it makes sense. It's time to get the final product that we can bring together.

*Problem:* What Easter game should we bring to market?
*Answer:* A soft, stuffed jellybean bag, folded cardboard, $5.95.
*Evaluation:* A cardboard game board that has Easter images and lines drawn on it. Jellybean bags are tossed, and points are scored based on where it falls on the cardboard game board. Sells during Easter season for $5.95.

Finally, we need to use our intuition to see if it will sell. It's not always just about coming up with a product to bring to market; it's also about determining whether it will sell. Normally, I would use a blend of analytics and intuition, but I would begin by tuning in.

**Problem:** Will this game sell?

**Answer:** I see children laughing and holding the game, bright spring sunshine, happy families.

**Evaluation:** I believe it will sell during the prime market time for Easter. Families will enjoy it for the day.

We have now successfully created the next great product to bring to market. By asking the questions and allowing the answers to come with no judgment, we have invented a new game. It has not yet been fully designed, but the concept has been fleshed out. It was conceived in an extremely simple but fruitful way, in a matter of five minutes, and can ultimately bring success to your company.

By utilizing our intuition, we are able to access the flow of desire that is currently in the universe. We have literally tapped into the stream of consciousness by using our metaphysical abilities. Remember, we are all connected through energy. It is this energy that has provided us with the answers necessary to generate a new product for today's current culture. More than that, we've seen, in our mind's eye, that the consumer will purchase it. What could be easier? What could be better? Trust your vibes—it will prove to you that it is real. By actualizing your visions, you will be the fierce success you know you can be!

## Make Them Want It

You've already learned how you can determine what types of products to market and even how to market them. Now it's time to understand how to make consumers want what you are selling. To begin with, you need to put the energy out in the universe. Once you've done that, you create a desire, the need for the public or your specific part of the community to want that product.

Now, how to create the longing for the product you are releasing into society? Imagine drawing a circle around your product or service. Now imagine concentric circles traveling outward from your product. As you watch the circles, imagine them going further, all the way out into the universe to connect to all the potential customers. See a heart pulsing within the circles, filled with love and desire.

You can continue sending it out for as long as your product is out there—it's like combining your intuitive awareness with your manifesting abilities. You have now completed the cycle. You've determined who your market is, and you've created and promoted the product. You can sit back and let it happen.

## Real-Life Money Decisions

We are dealing in real life. We will have real-life decisions to make and we have to trust, beyond reproach, that we are making good ones. Real life doesn't play around—it lets you know it's there and is ready to make you or break you.

My friend Lynn is an author. I swear she channels a book a week. She decided to self-publish her books. The first year she made next to nothing. The second she brought home $500. This was okay, she figured, for now. Lynn and her husband both had full-time jobs. Lynn was writing every waking moment that she wasn't working. Her husband was helping edit her books. They decided that something had to give. Lynn was close to earning her full pension, so she didn't want to leave her job. The question was, should her husband quit his job to become Lynn's full-time editor, or should he keep working and let the book editing suffer? They needed to make a choice, but it was driven by the concern of whether Lynn's books would sell enough to cover her husband's salary should he leave his current job. So far, it hadn't seemed like it.

She tuned in to her intuition. She really tuned in. She felt a sense of peace that everything would be fine if her husband quit his job. She felt the universe would provide for them and knew in her heart, intuitively, that it was a good idea. She wasn't nervous—she was actually okay with the idea of losing his income. She wasn't sure why, but she was certain all would work out. She was sending a beacon out to the world to create a demand for her books. She knew, intuitively, they would sell. She told him to go for it!

Well, that year her $500 check turned into a $150,000 income, seemingly out of the blue. It sounds unbelievable but it's true. She was totally shocked as it was definitely unexpected. Her books took off, and they more than made up for the lack of her husband's salary. She had had no valid evidence telling her she would be able to cover the income gap. In fact, everything signaled just the opposite. Her sales the two years prior had been minimal. Tuning in to her intuition had convinced her all would be okay. Apparently, it was more than okay—sales were booming. Her instincts had helped her sales, and I am convinced that by Lynn trusting her gut, the universe took care of them.

Knowing how to influence the people buying from you is crucial to your operating at a profit. You need to start by employing all the tools at your disposal, including your six sensory tools. You are in this to win it. Intuiting who you are dealing with and what makes them tick will help you get into their headspace to convince them they want what you've got. Blunt but true. Make use of everything you have and exploit what you perceive to your advantage, in a good way. Make them need what you are selling because you have figured out how it will benefit them by using your gut instincts, your intuition, to determine how it matches their wishes. And, then, sell the hell out of it.

Combining your cognitive with your intuitive skills can be the perfect balance. It can be just what you need to bring about a complete picture and an entire on-target plan to increase your sales and better your marketing. You don't have to start off knowing you will succeed, but you will definitely come to find out. Don't sell yourself short. You've come so far by utilizing your innate gifts. It's time you begin to truly get ahead.

# Wrapping It Up

When you put your intuition to work, you are telling yourself and those around you that you are smart enough to use every possible tool available to you. You could have just continued the way you were going. No one would fault you for that. Heck, people would probably admire your drive and determination to better yourself and your business world. I mean, after all, if you've read this book, you've probably already resolved yourself to getting ahead. You've most certainly got a grit to you, a resolute ambition to make something out of your life, because you have passion. You are motivated to thrive.

You've discovered your intuitive gifts and maybe you are humbled by them. Maybe you are also becoming even more successful. It is important to stay humble. Allowing your gifts to make you feel like you're better than everyone else or using them to manipulate others can actually limit them. Remember, the universe is conspiring for you to succeed, but it does not want you to neglect every bit of humanity you have. It is important to remain modest and respectful of others. That doesn't negate the prosperous person you have developed into, but it does allow you to stay real.

Chances are you've tried other programs or other methods, and your reward may have been less than what you'd hoped for, but you've persevered. You've continued striving and hustling, but now you are walking away with a greater gift then you could have imagined. You have tapped into the one thing that is truly yours to utilize your entire life and that you can continue to develop. You've been turned on to the opportunities you can take advantage of, but what if you need more help to move forward? There's no limit to how far you can go, and finding someone who knows how to help you can be priceless.

## Finding the Right Teacher to Further Your Intuition

There are so many self-help gurus out there; hopefully, the information in this book will help you determine what type of person will be right for you and what areas you are looking to further develop. There are teachers who are completely legitimate, have studied how to use their tools to really help you, and have created an (almost) perfected programs and exercises to help you become the best you you can be. And then you have the other ones— those that are, how shall we say it, complete quacks just out to make a quick buck by ripping you off, spouting knowledge they've copied from others, or charging you a gazillion dollars to attend a workshop with them and hold hands with a bunch of other people who have paid a gazillion dollars to do the same thing.

The funny thing is that either way, if it works, then it's worth it. I say this because any time you are challenged to examine your gifts, it can help you. If you're able to look beyond what the teachers are saying, it can bring you closer to the level of ability you want to achieve because you are utilizing your skills. You will always learn when you do that, regardless of how good or bad the teacher is. But what tools have you taken away to continue that same feeling or to use to help you reach your goals? Do the teachers or leaders have a background in what they are imparting to you as priceless wisdom? Or have they simply decided they can do it because others can? Sometimes it's hard to tell the difference.

Often, the proof is in the pudding. What have they taught you that you didn't already know? More importantly, how do they make you feel? If it was too easy or you found yourself yawning throughout much of the workshop, maybe you're already way ahead of where they are in your development. If it felt yucky (and by yucky, I mean made your skin crawl) and made you feel like you wanted to vomit, they probably weren't the right trainer for you. But if they make you feel elated, like even though what they were telling you to do may have scared you, you felt like you could relate and truly grab ahold of the basic concepts and ideas they shared, then they might be a good fit. These people, the ones who have philosophies that may possibly challenge you, but in a good way, are the educators you need. These are the coaches who will elevate your game and hopefully help coax your awesome self out from underneath all your insecurities and doubts.

Essentially, in order to learn more, go deeper, and take away an increased awareness, you want to raise the level of your knowledge. This in turn will increase your proficiency. Whether you do that through your own research and practice or you take advantage of the great teachers who are available to you, you will find yourself opening up to your clair skills. The more you exercise your gifts, the more routine it will become to employ them. You may find yourself repeating one method habitually or making use of all the clairs to tune in to your inner guidance system, but the approach will be the same—you just have to begin!

## Remember to Believe in Your Abilities

It's possible you didn't believe in your extrasensory gifts before reading this book. But now that you do, you will probably discover you don't want to stop using what is a beneficial and even profitable method of gathering information. The techniques you use are up to you. You can practice with the exercises in this and my other books. Mix it up a bit by checking out books by other authors as well. You might find you are ready to seek out a mentor or teacher to take you to that next level in your self-discovery. Perhaps you'll decide following your own journey through meditation or just intentionally tuning in to a specific situation using your clair abilities is the way you want to proceed. Regardless of the process, you have begun your quest for the knowledge your awareness can bring you.

Intuition shows up in so many areas of your life; listening to it will always help you. From your personal life to your career, everything is better when you pay attention to what's inside you, to your natural gifts. When you don't respect your sixth sensory gifts, it can feel like you are drowning. Everything will feel upended, and eventually that can lead to emotional upheaval. Ultimately, you are the guardian of your gifts, and you are the only one in charge of when you tune in to them.

Trusting your senses is the opening to a world filled with opportunities. It creates an upward trajectory, leading you toward becoming the person you are meant to be. It can help you with decisions and present you with a more fulfilling life. It will aid you in taking chances without as much risk since you have the support of your metaphysical senses and can continually build your business with forward momentum. Your ESP brings with it an enhanced creativity, as well as a deeper connection with coworkers, staff, and relationships.

Believing in your intuition can allow you to trust others. It gives you an instant sense of right or wrong, good or bad. The more you learn to trust it, the more often it will help you. When you go with your gut instincts, you'll almost always head down the right path and land right-side up, and maybe with some new friends.

There is no limit to the benefits of utilizing your amazing gifts. It is up to you to learn how your intuition works for you. It is also your choice whether you decide to use it or not, but by now I'm hoping you will have determined that there is absolutely no downside! Leveraging your intuition means using this gift to your advantage. You use all your other tools to get ahead in life, so leveraging your intuition is a logical progression. You've read this book all the way through. You know how it works. More specifically, you have done some of the work or thought about your answers.

*You know this is real and you also know now that you are totally*
*ready to put your intuition to work and thrive!*
*Congratulations—there's no way to go but up!*

# Bibliography

Bennis, Warren. *On Becoming a Leader: The Leadership Classic.* Philadelphia, PA: Basic Books, 2009.

Brandon, Diane. *Intuition for Beginners: Easy Ways to Awaken Your Natural Abilities.* Woodbury, MN: Llewellyn Publications, 2013.

Castrillon, Caroline. "3 Ways Entrepreneurs Can Tap into Their Intuition to Get That Extra Edge." *Forbes*, May 29, 2019. https://www.forbes.com /sites/carolinecastrillon/2019/05/29/3-ways-entrepreneurs-can-tap -into-their-intuition-to-get-that-extra-edge/#3c7889c758bd.

Chopra, Deepak. "How to Change Your Energy." Oprah.com. November 4, 2009. https://www.oprah.com/spirit/how-to-change-your-energy/all.

Coelho, Paulo. *The Alchemist.* 25th anniversary edition. New York: Harper-One, 2014.

Crummy, Colin. "Is It Healthy to Obsess over a Nemesis? Stylist Investigates." Stylist. Accessed July 27, 2020. https://www.stylist.co.uk/life/is-it -healthy-to-obsesses-over-a-nemesis/320226.

Day, Laura. *Practical Intuition: How to Harness the Power of Your Instinct and Make It Work for You.* New York: Broadway Books, 1997.

———. *Practical Intuition for Success: A Step-by-Step Program to Increase Your Wealth Today.* New York: HarperCollins Publishers, 1997.

Dillard, Sherrie: *Discover Your Psychic Type: Developing and Using Your Natural Intuition.* Woodbury, MN: Lewellyn Publications, 2008.

———. *You Are Psychic: Develop Your Natural Intuition through Your Psychic Type.* Woodbury: Llewellyn Publications, 2018.

Dourado, Phil. *The 60 Second Leader: Everything You Need to Know About Leadership, in 60 Second Bites.* Chichester, UK: Capstone Books, 2007.

Dyer, Wayne W. "Manifesting 101: The Art of Creating a Life You Love." Dr. Wayne W. Dyer. November 9, 2015. https://www.drwaynedyer.com/blog/manifesting-101-mastering-the-art-of-getting-what-you-want/.

Eden, Donna, and David Feinstein. *Energy Medicine: Balancing Your Body's Energies for Optimal Health, Joy, and Vitality.* Toronto: Tarcher Perigee, 2008.

Gibran, Kahlil. *Sand and Foam: A Book of Aphorisms.* New York: Knopf, 2011.

Hansen O'Neill, Heather. *Find Your Fire at Forty: Creating A Joyful Life During the Age of Discontent.* Garden City, NY: Morgan James Publishing, 2011.

Ibarra, Herminia. *Act Like a Leader, Think Like a Leader.* Boston, MA: Harvard Business Review Press, 2015.

Jobs, Steve. Stanford University Commencement Address, June 12, 2005. https://news.stanford.edu/2005/06/14/jobs-061505/.

Johnson, Vic. *It's Never Too Late and You're Never Too Old: 50 People Who Found Success After 50.* Melrose, FL: Laurenzana Press, 2013.

K., Lisa. *Intuition on Demand: A Step-By-Step Guide to Powerful Intuition You Can Trust.* Forres, Scotland: Findhorn Press, 2017.

Koontz, Dean. *The Darkest Evening of the Year.* New York: Bantam Dell, 2008.

Margolis, Char. *Discover Your Inner Wisdom: Using Intuition, Logic, and Common Sense to Make Your Best Choices.* New York: Fireside, 2008.

McLeod, Lisa Earle. "How to Leverage Intuition in Decision-Making." Huff-Post. Last modified November 24, 2014. https://www.huffpost.com/entry/how-to-leverage-intuition_b_5868488.

Ragan, Lynn. *Signs from the Afterlife: Identifying Gifts from the Other Side.* Atlanta, GA: Self-published, 2014.

Snyder, Rick. *Decisive Intuition: Use Your Gut Instincts to Make Smart Business Decisions*. Newburyport, MA: Career Press, 2019.

Wright, Simone. "Using Our Dreams as Intuitive messengers." HuffPost. Last modified December 30, 2014. https://www.huffpost.com/entry/using-our-dreams-as-intui_b_6057292.

## To Write to the Author

If you wish to contact the author or would like more information about this book, please write to the author in care of Llewellyn Worldwide Ltd. and we will forward your request. Both the author and the publisher appreciate hearing from you and learning of your enjoyment of this book and how it has helped you. Llewellyn Worldwide Ltd. cannot guarantee that every letter written to the author can be answered, but all will be forwarded. Please write to:

Melanie Barnum
℅ Llewellyn Worldwide
2143 Wooddale Drive
Woodbury, MN 55125-2989

Please enclose a self-addressed stamped envelope for reply,
or $1.00 to cover costs. If outside the U.S.A., enclose
an international postal reply coupon.

Many of Llewellyn's authors have websites with additional information and resources. For more information, please visit our website at http://www .llewellyn.com.